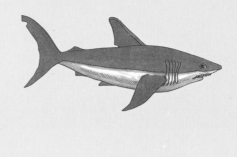

What causes twins?   •   **Who was Harry Houdini?**   •   **Are all sharks dangerous?**   •

Who was Jackie Robinson?   •   **What is a meteor?**   •   **Who was Queen Elizabeth I?**   •

How do plants eat?   •   **How do spiders spin webs?**   •   **What are chicken pox?**   •

When was the first car invented?   •   **How does an electric guitar work?**   •

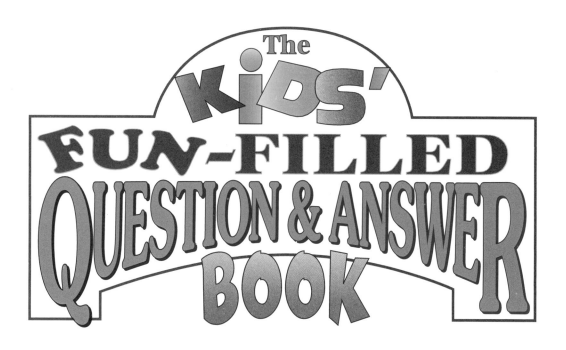

The Kids' FUN-FILLED QUESTION & ANSWER BOOK

Text by
Jane Parker Resnick

Illustrated by
Tony Tallarico

kidsbooks Incorporated

ABOUT THIS BOOK
Note to Parents and Teachers

GETTING CHILDREN'S ATTENTION

The Kid's Fun-Filled Question & Answer Book is a unique learning tool, one that is specially created to stimulate and educate young children. The book's humorous illustrations, coupled with a wealth of fascinating facts, will draw children into the world of learning—and keep them there!

SPARKING THEIR INTEREST

The Kids' Fun-Filled Question & Answer Book is designed to draw out the natural curiosity inside of every young child. By presenting questions in a format that is exciting and fun, this book not only provides fact-filled answers, but also encourages children to ask questions of their own. And the more questions kids ask, the more interested they will become in the world around them.

THE QUESTIONS IN THIS BOOK

The questions in *The Kids' Fun-Filled Question & Answer Book* are educationally sound (What is the world's most populated city?) but also fun and unique (What's the smelliest thing in the world?). They are meant to provide young children with important knowledge while inspiring them to be thoughtful and curious. In addition, the hilarious illustrations animate the information in a way that no ordinary reference book can. Topics include the natural world, outer space, the human body, inventions, wonders of science, and much more.

BUILDING AN AT-HOME LIBRARY

An at-home library is best when it contains informational resources that are both educational and fun to read. *The Kids' Fun-Filled Dictionary*, *The Kids' Fun-Filled Encyclopedia*, and *The Kids' Fun-Filled Questions & Answer Book* do just that. They keep kids learning—and laughing!

How many people live in the world?

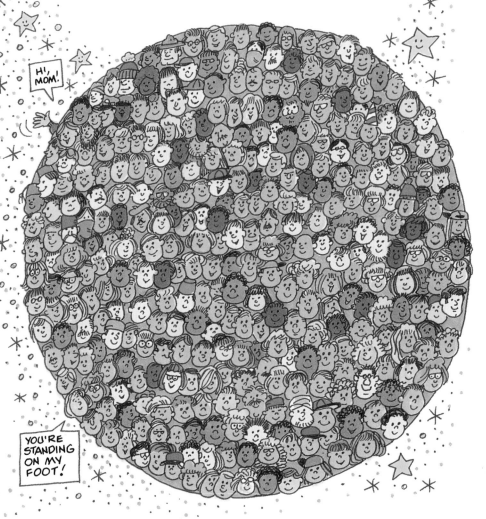

In 1994, the population of the world was over five and a half billion. In the year 2020, scientists estimate close to 8 billion. In that same year, China's population will probably grow to almost one and a half billion, about one fifth of all the people in the world!

How deep is the ocean?

In the Pacific Ocean, in the Mariana Trench near the Philippines, the sea's floor plunges to 36,198 feet—that's nearly 7 miles deep! The ocean's bottom is dark and cold, but it's not flat. There are mountains more than 12,000 feet high under all that water.

How tall is the world's tallest living tree?

A giant redwood in the Humboldt National Forest in California is the tallest tree on Earth. How tall is it? You could look out the top-floor window of a building 30 stories high—and still not see the top. At last measurement, in October 1991, it was 365 feet tall.

What makes a skunk smell?

That ghastly spray is the skunk's best defense and, boy, does it work! No creature, human or beast, can stand being near a skunk with that odor. It comes from a fluid called musk which is produced and stored in a pair of glands under the animal's tail. A skunk can propel the spray about 10 feet!

When were comic books invented?

Comic books are single square newspaper cartoons that have grown up. From cartoons came comic strips, which are three or four squares long. The first comic book as we know it was *Famous Funnies,* which first appeared in 1934. The first comic book super-hero, *Superman,* landed on news-stands in 1939.

What is the Loch Ness Monster?

Now you see it, now you don't! In 1933, a couple claimed they saw a dinosaur-like monster in Loch Ness, a lake in Scotland. Three thousand sightings of "Nessie" have occurred since, but none of them has proven the creature's existence for sure!

Why do people snore?

If someone catches you snoring, blame your uvula (OOV-you-la). It's a small piece of flesh at the back of the throat that hangs down from the roof of the mouth. Sometimes air from the lungs causes the uvula to vibrate—and that's the snoring sound. It happens most often when you breathe through your mouth.

What makes the wind blow?

The air around the Earth is unevenly heated by the sun. Hot air surrounds the equator, cold air hangs over the North and South Poles. Warm air rises and cold air sinks, and this movement creates wind. Movement in one place causes movement in another, just the way if you pour a cup of water into a full bucket, all the water swirls and moves. This is how patterns of wind cross the Earth's surface.

HA-HA!
HEE-HEE!
HO-HO!

Why are feet so ticklish?

Nerve endings are what make us feel ticklish. And the more nerve endings there are in a particular spot, the more ticklish it is. Our feet have the most nerve endings—so they're the most ticklish of all!

How big is the biggest diamond in the world?

Diamonds, like other gems, are measured in carats. (Not carrots, those are for rabbits.) A carat weighs 0.2 grams. The largest fine quality, colorless diamond ever found was called "The Cullinan." It was mined in South Africa and weighed 3,106 carats. It was cut into 106 jewels and produced the finest, largest gemstone ever, weighing 530.2 carats.

What is octopus ink?

It's a smoke screen. When threatened, an octopus discharges a thick blackish or brownish inky fluid which is stored in its body. The ejected ink doesn't dissolve quickly. It floats in the water in a cloud shaped somewhat like an octopus. The idea is to confuse its enemies and cover its escape—and it works.

Who invented *pizza?*

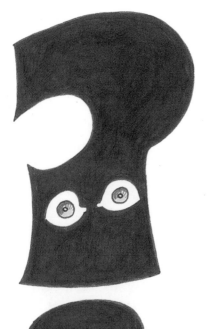

Pizza was first cooked up in the kitchens of Naples, Italy, about 500 years ago. No one person created it. It was just something a lot of people ate around Naples. The Duke of Naples made pizza popular by adding a variety of toppings. Without cheese and tomato sauce toppings, pizza is just plain crusty dough.

Why can't I see in the dark?

The human eye uses light to see. Light bounces off your surroundings and into your eye through your pupil, the black hole at the center. A picture forms on your retina, the lining at the back of the eye. Your brain makes sense out of what you see. Without light, there is nothing to enter your retina and start the whole process going.

What is ESP?

ESP stands for **E**xtra **S**ensory **P**erception. Regular sensory perception is the way we see the world through our five senses—sight, hearing, smell, taste, and touch. But "extra" goes beyond into the realm of seeing the *unseen*. That could include looking through walls, hearing the voices of dead people, or getting a strong feeling about something that is going to happen in the future.

Why is it considered unlucky to open an umbrella indoors?

Umbrellas were first used by African royalty to shield themselves from the hot rays of the sun god. To open one in the shade insulted the god. To open one indoors must have been worse, probably punishable by the god. Today, we think of it as just plain unlucky.

HOW DO CLOUDS FORM?

Millions of water droplets together form clouds. They start out as *water vapor*, the evaporated water that rises from lakes, oceans, rivers, and plants. Water vapor cools as it rises into the air and, as the temperature drops, it changes to liquid. These masses of tiny water droplets form clouds. When the clouds get too heavy, they fall to Earth as rain. They flow into lakes and rivers...and the whole process begins all over again.

ARE THERE ANY REAL CASTLES IN THE WORLD?

Think of your house as your castle. The kings, queens, and nobles of the Middle Ages did. Their castles were their homes, the places where they lived. But castles were also symbols of their power, and fortresses against rivals who might try to make war on them. These grand homes were built between the ninth and the fifteenth centuries all over Europe. Many have been preserved—and you can visit them. They're mostly hotels or museums now.

WHAT IS STONEHENGE?

Stonehenge is a mystery—on a grand scale. An enormous ancient monument, Stonehenge was built in southern England over 3,000 years ago. The monument consists of many large stones, some weighing up to 100,000 pounds, arranged in circular patterns. It may have been used to observe the movements of the sun and moon—and then to create calendars. No one really knows.

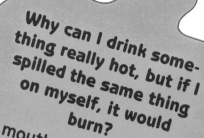

Why can I drink some-thing really hot, but if I spilled the same thing on myself, it would burn?

Your mouth has air-conditioning! As you sip a hot liquid, air comes into your mouth along with it and cools the drink. Your saliva mixes in and cools it fur-ther. But hot stuff on your skin is just plain hot!

Who wrote the song
"Happy Birthday to You"?

The Hill girls, Mildred and Patty, wrote "Good Morning to You" in 1893. The song was not a big hit until someone changed the words at a birthday party. No one knows exactly who made the change. There aren't many words, but for birthdays, four is all you need:
Happy Birthday to You!

What's the difference between a dolphin and a porpoise?

Their facial structure and body size. Both are mammals, not fish, and have to breathe above water. Both are related to whales, but are smaller. Dolphins can grow to 12 feet in length and have a beak. Porpoises are beakless and are usually between three and six feet long.

WE'RE MAMMAL COUSINS.

-46 -47 -48 -49- 50-51 - 52-53 - 54-55-56-

WHAT'S THE DIFFERENCE BETWEEN AN INSECT AND A SPIDER ?

Look out for legs. Spiders have eight. Insects have six. Also check out the antennae. Insects have them and spiders don't. Up close (if you dare), look at the number of body parts. Insects have three. Spiders have two. And if the animal is hanging by a thread, it's a spider. Spiders make silk. Insects don't.

How fast do a hummingbird's wings beat?

Faster than you can see. Hummingbirds, the smallest feathered creatures on the planet, are also the fastest wing-beaters. The beating is so speedy it looks like a blur. With a slow motion camera, it can almost be counted—50 to 75 beats per second! Hummingbirds can even fly backwards, something no other bird can do.

WHY DO ZEBRAS AND TIGERS HAVE STRIPES?

Camouflage—to help them hide. If a zebra or a tiger were in your backyard, you'd know it. But if you were in their neighborhood, you might miss them. Striped coats are hard to see in the light and dark shadows of forests and grasslands. This helps to keep them safe from predators. Now you see them. Now you don't!

The vibration of shell-like rings on the end of its tail. The rattle is made up of dry, hard pieces of unshed skin. As the snake grows, the number of rings increases. So, the louder the rattle, the bigger the snake. The snake will shake its rattles to tell an intruder to..."Take off!"

What makes a rattlesnake's tail rattle?

I'M GOING OUT!

Why does a match light up?

In a word—friction. Matches were the accidental discovery of John Walker, a chemist. In 1827, he was trying to produce a burnable material for shotguns. His first match was a stick he was using to stir a mixture of chemicals. It burst into flames when he scraped it against a stone floor to clean off the end.

What causes an eclipse of the sun?

When the moon moves directly between the Earth and the sun, the sun's light is blocked and the moon's shadow falls on the Earth for a short time. This is called a *solar eclipse*. For a *total eclipse*, you would have to be lined up exactly with the full shadow of the moon. Otherwise, you'd see only a portion of the eclipse—a *partial eclipse*.

When were roller skates invented?

Talk about an entrance! To introduce his invention, Joseph Merlin of Huy, Belgium, roller-skated into a ballroom playing the violin. That was in 1759. Unfortunately, he didn't know how to stop and crashed into a full-length mirror, breaking his violin.

Who invented money?

The first piece of metal to be considered a coin was invented in Lydia, Turkey, around 670 B.C. But the idea of money took shape over a long time. People traded ten chickens for a cow, or a basket of berries for six ears of corn. But what if the person with the berries wanted wheat instead of corn? Or what if the owner of the berries left them at home? Eventually, it made sense to have something that always had the same value and was easy to carry. And that something was money.

WHAT IS GLASS MADE OF?

OOPS!

Glass starts out being soft and syrupy. It's a mixture of sand, soda, and lime melted together at high temperatures. In this state it can be shaped into the glass objects we see around us. Various minerals can be added to make different colored glass. Then, the "syrup" is cooled, heated, and cooled again in a process that makes it hard.

How many stars are there in the Milky Way?

About 100 billion, and our sun is only one of them. The Milky Way is a spiral galaxy, which means it's shaped a little like a Frisbee. Earth lies somewhere between the center and one edge. Light, which travels at a speed of six trillion miles per year, takes about 100,000 years to go from one end of the Milky Way to the other.

3,050,043,
3,050,044,
3,050,045,
3,050,046,
3,050,047...

DID HE COUNT US YET?

I'M HEADING FOR THE MILKY WAY!

STOP PUSHING!

THIS IS A GRADE "A" GALAXY.

What makes popcorn pop?

Every kernel of corn has a tiny droplet of water in it. Heat the kernel, and the water turns to steam. Steam takes up more space than water, so it presses against the walls of the kernel. The corn expands and expands and...explodes! Poppppp!

IT MUST HAVE BEEN THE POPCORN!

HIC-HIC-HIC-HIC-HIC-HIC-HIC-HIC-

STAND CLEAR FOR POPPING POPCORN

IT'S A BLAST!

THANK YOU,

I LIKE POPCORN!

WHY DO I GET THE HICCUPS?

It all starts with your diaphragm, the big muscle below your lungs. Usually, the diaphragm works smoothly, expanding and contracting your lungs. But if it gets irritated, perhaps by eating too quickly, it pulls down sharply. Air whooshes into your lungs...Hic! To keep too much air from entering your lungs, a small flap at the top of your windpipe snaps shut...Cup!

I'M ON A DIET!

What is the most powerful muscle in my body?

Your jaw muscle—and it's because exercise makes muscles stronger! Talking and chewing exercise this muscle more than any other.

HOW MANY KINDS OF INSECTS ARE THERE?

More than one million different species! They are by far the largest group in the animal world. They've been breaking up picnics for about 400 million years almost everywhere on the planet. There are more kinds of beetles and weevils—over 300,000—than any other type of insect.

How do you make potato chips?

Deep-fat frying is the good old-fashioned way. Slice some potatoes as thinly as possible. Soak them in cold water for two hours, changing the water twice. Drain them and dry them carefully with paper towels. In a deep pot, bring some cooking oil to a high heat. Drop the potato slices into the hot oil. Shake and stir, cooking them until they're golden. Drain them on paper towels and eat. Delicious! If you want to try making your own potato chips, ask an adult for some help!

How do whales talk?

They sing! Or to be specific, male humpback whales do. The songs of the humpbacks are a form of communication much stronger than the human voice. Underwater, whales send messages heard several miles away. Whales make sounds with a system of tubes and air sacs around their blow-holes. Squeaks and whistles and strange moaning are what whale songs sound like to humans. The songs of male humpbacks have been taped. People listen to these record-ings as they would any other kind of music.

Why do flamingos stand on one leg?

Instinct has taught flamingos good body mechanics. Standing on one leg and then the other gives each limb a chance to rest and keep warm.

Do animals use tools?

Some do. The woodpecker finch of the Galapagos Islands uses a tool to dig insects out of holes. The bird uses a cactus spine, which it holds in its beak. Apes use twigs and blades of grass to hunt insects. Seabirds use rocks. They drop clams and other hard-shelled sea creatures against the hard rocks to split open their shells.

HOW DOES AN ELECTRIC GUITAR WORK?

Play an electric guitar and you're actually producing sound with an amplifier and a loudspeaker, not a set of strings. Each metal string is attached to a pick-up, which is a small coil of wire with magnets set in it. The pick-up sends an electrical signal to the amplifier, then to the loudspeaker, and right to your audience.

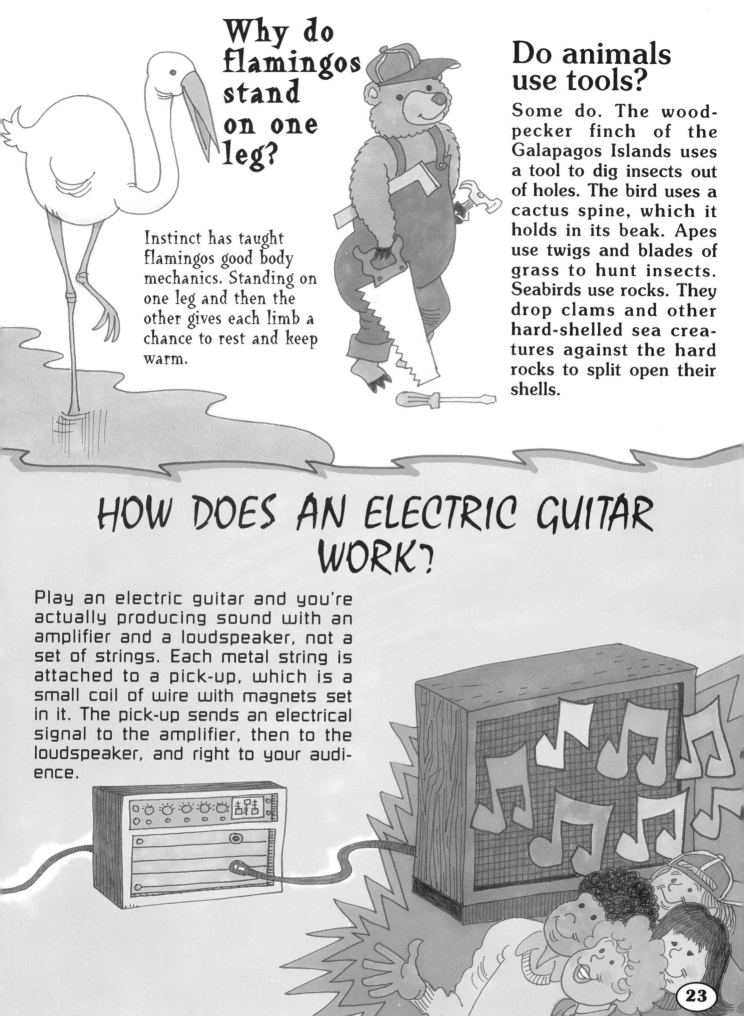

23

Who invented Silly Putty™?

In the 1940s, James Wright was an engineer whose assignment was to try and make a substitute for synthetic rubber. It never worked because the "rubber" stretched and bounced and didn't keep its form. But Wright liked this funny substance and kept it around. In 1949, a toy store owner bought a large amount and sold one-ounce balls in plastic eggs. Silly Putty™ was born.

What's the difference between a tortoise and a turtle?

A tortoise lives on land. It has clubbed feet like an elephant and a shell that is high-domed and thick. The largest tortoises can be 500 pounds. The turtle is a water creature with legs that resemble flippers. Leatherback turtles, by far the largest turtle, can grow to eight feet and weigh 1,500 pounds!

HOW DO YOU MAKE CARTOONS?

Bugs Bunny bites a carrot. Beauty kisses the Beast. The movement looks natural, but it's really made up of hundreds of *still* drawings. These drawings are flipped very fast in a row—24 per second! The speed gives the illusion of movement. How are the drawings "flipped?" Using a special high-speed camera called a pixilation camera. Today, computers also help make the still drawings "move."

How does a caterpillar turn into a butterfly?

It's not a miracle . . . it's *metamorphosis*, which means "change of form." A butterfly begins life as an egg, which grows into a caterpillar. After a period of maturing, a hard shell called a *chrysalis* develops over the caterpillar. Inside, the creature's body gradually changes. The shell breaks open, and out comes a lovely butterfly.

WHAT'S IT LIKE AT THE BOTTOM OF THE OCEAN?

The deeper you go, the darker it gets. Many fish who live at 2,000 feet or deeper have their own flashlights. They are *luminous*—they glow with light-producing cells. This light helps them get around in the blackness and attract prey. Other fish are blind—since they can't see down there, they never developed functioning eyes. Most of all, it's *cold* at the bottom—sometimes as cold as 28 degrees Fahrenheit.

HI!

25

What was the first tool?

In 1976, scientists found a chopper made of stone in Ethiopia in Africa. They believe that the object was made by early humans around 2.7 million years ago. It would have been handy for digging, scraping, or hacking.

How do evergreens stay green all year?

It's due to the shape of their leaves—or needles. Trees take up water through their roots. The water evaporates into the air through their leaves. Trees with flat, broad leaves lose a lot of water. In winter, when the ground is frozen, these trees shed their leaves to hold on to their water supply. But evergreens have needle-like leaves with a thick, waxy covering. These needles don't lose much moisture, so they remain on the tree. After a few years, they fall off, but new ones grow in at the same time, so the tree is *ever green!*

How can a parrot talk?

By repeating the "nonsense" sounds it hears over and over and over again. When a parrot says "Polly wants a cracker," it doesn't have a cracker in mind. The bird can't understand what it's saying. But it can learn to make the sounds by practicing. In the same way, you could learn to say a few sentences in a foreign language you didn't know.

I DON'T LIKE CRACKERS!

How do bees make honey?

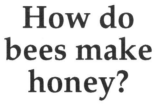

It all starts with nectar, the sugary juice of flowers that honeybees bring back to the hive. In the hive, worker bees add important enzymes (or chemicals) from their bodies to the nectar and deposit it in the honeycombs. Then, special bees fan this nectar with their wings. The heat of the hive and the fanning make some of the water in the nectar evaporate, and turn it into honey.

How does a sprouting seed know which way is up?

WHICH WAY IS UP?

Gravity gives the seed directions. Tiny nodules in the growing tips of seeds respond to gravity so that the roots are pulled downward. That way, the shoots will always point up.

How old is the universe?

Fifteen billion years is the estimate. The big mystery is how the universe began. One important theory is the Big Bang. Some scientists believe that all matter was once a single mass. Then an enormous explosion sent pieces flying off into space, creating galaxies and planets and stars. The theory says that the galaxies are all still moving away from each other because of the force of that explosion billions of years ago. But other scientists think things have always been pretty much the same.

HAPPY BIRTHDAY!!

LOOK AT THAT!!

What is a meteor?

Meteors have more than one name, just like people. Particles of matter or pieces of rock that fall through space are called meteoroids. If they burn up in the Earth's atmosphere, they are called meteors. Most of them burn into nothing and are never seen again, but if they survive and hit the ground, they become meteorites and form big craters where they land.

WHY DO WE SNEEZE?

Your nose knows. Anything that gets in your nose, like dust or germs, is something your body doesn't want. You sneeze to get rid of it. The big A-Choo! is air from your lungs that comes up, shoots rapidly through your nose, and clears it.

Who was Mozart?

Wolfgang Amadeus Mozart was one of the world's youngest musicians. He was born in Austria in 1756 and composed his first piece for a full symphony orchestra at the age of five! He also performed. During his lifetime, he created many symphonies, concertos, and operas—some of the most beautiful music ever written. And he lived only 35 years.

Why is a four leaf clover considered LUCKY?

Legends about the four leaf clover go all the way back to Adam and Eve. It is said that Eve took a four leaf clover when she was sent from the Garden of Eden. A piece of green from the world's first garden spot must be something rare and wonderful—special enough to bring good luck.

Why does the sky change color from red at dawn to blue during the day?

The sun's white light is actually made up of many colors—red, orange, yellow, green, blue, indigo, and violet. When light comes through the atmosphere and is scattered by dust particles, the various different shades of light are separated. Which one we see depends on how thick the layer of dust is and where the sun may be. During the day, when the sun is high in the sky, blue light is scattered the most. At dusk and dawn, when the sun is near the horizon, we see it through a much thicker layer of dust. The red and orange light comes through most, and the sky gets fiery.

WHO INVENTED NUMBERS?

Numbers are really ideas. We can't see them, so we create signs or symbols to represent them. The concept of numbers, and the symbols to represent them, developed when people needed to count things. Different civilizations used different kinds of numbers. The 1, 2, 3 type of numbers we use are called Arabic numerals. They were probably invented by the Hindus in India about 1,400 years ago. But it isn't the oldest system. The Babylonians invented a number system about 3,500 years ago.

How do bubbles get in fizzy drinks?

Nature didn't do it. Manufacturers give drinks the fizz that tickles your taste buds. First, they force carbon dioxide into the drink under pressure and seal the bottle or can. The gas stays in the liquid until you open the drink. Then . . . *whoosh! hiss!* . . . the carbon dioxide escapes. Where does it go? It's in the bubbles.

WHAT IS GRAVITY?

The big pull. Gravity is the force at the center of a planet that attracts other objects to it. The Earth's force of gravity keeps our feet on the ground. Gravity actually holds the universe together, too. The sun's gravity keeps the planets in their orbits. Without it, the Earth would shoot off into space.

HOW LONG HAVE ESCALATORS BEEN GOING UP AND DOWN?

About a century. Coney Island, New York, had the world's first escalator in 1896. In London in 1911, people were worried about putting their feet on that city's first moving stairs. So a man with a wooden leg was hired to take the ride and show that if a man with one leg could do it, the two-legged types had nothing to fear.

HOW DOES A FLYING FISH FLY?

Not like a bird. These small fish (the largest is about a foot and a half) propel themselves into the air with their tails and glide. Fear makes them do it. If a bigger fish is chasing them, they flap their tails, pick up speed, and leap out of the water. Then they spread their front fins and sail on the breeze—up to 20 miles per hour.

What happens when I dream?

You "see" your dreams with your eyes. Dream sleep is called REM sleep for Rapid Eye Movement because your eyes move behind your closed lids as if you were scanning a picture. Scientists think that dreaming is a way of sorting out and storing the happenings of the day.

Who invented indoor plumbing?

Someone we should all thank. On the Mediterranean island of Crete, a system was installed 4,000 years ago. Indoor plumbing requires pipes that bring water into the house and drainage pipes that take waste out. The flush toilet was invented by Sir John Harrington in 1589, but didn't reach its present form until the 1800s.

Why does a body sink in QUICKSAND ?

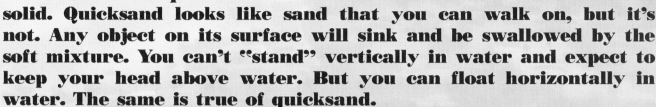

Because it is a mixture of water and sand and works more like a liquid than a solid. Quicksand looks like sand that you can walk on, but it's not. Any object on its surface will sink and be swallowed by the soft mixture. You can't "stand" vertically in water and expect to keep your head above water. But you can float horizontally in water. The same is true of quicksand.

What makes the Leaning Tower of Pisa lean?

The Leaning Tower of Pisa in northern Italy is a church bell tower. Its construction began in 1173, but was soon halted when the builders realized the 10-foot foundation wasn't deep enough to keep the tower from tilting in the soft soil. The 180-foot tower, weighing 16,000 tons, was finally completed 200 years later. To keep it from toppling over, the people of Pisa have repeatedly gone in and reinforced the foundation. But they haven't dared try to straighten the tower!

EVERYBODY— PULL TOGETHER!

UGH!

OOFF!

IT'S NOT MOVING!

Why do people have straight, wavy, or curly hair?

As a strand of hair grows, it squeezes through a tiny hole called a follicle. The shape of a person's follicles makes hair straight, wavy, or curly. Think of a toothpaste tube—if the opening weren't round, but shaped like a square or a star instead, the stream of toothpaste would look completely different. Straight hair grows out of round follicles, waves from oval follicles, and tight, round curls spring from square follicles!

Why do salmon and other fish swim upstream?

THIS WAY

Because they return to where they were born when they are ready to breed. And that can be a long way—sometimes thousands of miles. Salmon are born in rivers and streams and then travel to sea to live as adults. But instinct helps them find their way home. They swim against the current and even jump over waterfalls trying to find the exact spot where they were born.

What causes EARTHQUAKES?

THIS IS A GOOD TIME TO MAKE A MILKSHAKE!

The problem is underground. Pressure inside the Earth causes giant plates of rocks in the Earth's crust to shove against one another. When these rock plates collide, the Earth's surface cracks, and the ground shakes. The shock waves carry the shudders for miles, and the Earth *quakes*.

Who started April Fool's Day?

Silly days for practical jokes are found all around the world. Perhaps the day started with the French, who once began the new year on the first of April. In 1564, when the new calendar began the year with January 1, some people resisted. They were considered April fools.

What was the first movie?

In Paris, France, in 1895, Louis and Auguste Lumiere showed the first moving picture, a short film of workers leaving a factory. The first movie with a story was Edwin Porter's *The Great Train Robbery* in 1903. It was a sensation, but silent. In 1927, *The Jazz Singer* was the first full-length movie with sound.

THIS IS A SCENE FROM "THE GREAT TRAIN ROBBERY."

TODAY, THE TRAIN WOULD BE LATE!!

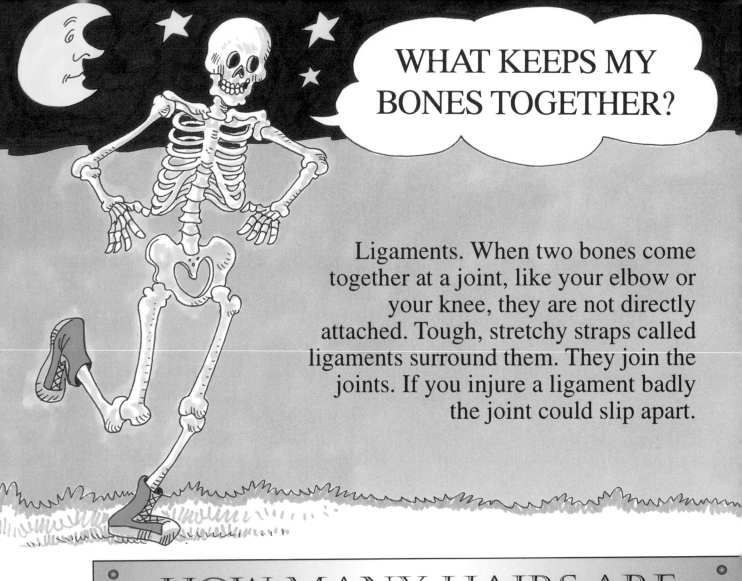

WHAT KEEPS MY BONES TOGETHER?

Ligaments. When two bones come together at a joint, like your elbow or your knee, they are not directly attached. Tough, stretchy straps called ligaments surround them. They join the joints. If you injure a ligament badly the joint could slip apart.

HOW MANY HAIRS ARE ON A PERSON'S HEAD?

I THINK I NEED A HAIRCUT!

The average is about 125,000 hairs, but they would be very hard to count. Head hair is always falling out and growing in. About 50 to 75 hairs fall out each day.

WHAT GIVES MY EYES THEIR COLOR?

The iris. The iris surrounds the pupil, the opening at the center, and controls the amount of light that passes through the hole. The back of the iris has pigment—called melanin—that protects it from light. This is the color we see. If you have blue or green-colored eyes, the iris has small amounts of melanin. Larger amounts of the pigment give you brown or hazel eyes.

WHAT ARE TEARS FOR?

Tears are cleaning fluid for the eye. They come from the lacrimal glands, which sit above the outer edge of each eye. And tears keep coming. Every time you blink, they cover your eye and wash away dirt and germs. When you cry, tears may help you get rid of extra chemicals that build up in your body.

WHAT CAUSES AN ALLERGY?

A mistake. Your body has an army to defend you against germs. The main soldiers are white cells, which create antibodies to attack specific germs. But sometimes the white cells act as if harmless foreign substances, like dust or pollen, are dangerous. They cause your nose to run, your eyes to tear, and your skin to itch.

THIS IS NOT MY DAY!

SNIFF-SNIFF!

How many different kinds of rocks are there?

ONLY THREE?

Even though rocks are everywhere, they are all variations of only three basic kinds. *Sedimentary* rocks, like limestone, are formed near the surface of the Earth when erosion causes sand, pebbles, and shells to get buried in layers. *Igneous* rocks, like granite, were once liquid lava which cooled to hardness. *Metamorphic* rocks, like slate, are sedimentary or igneous rocks changed by underground heat and pressure.

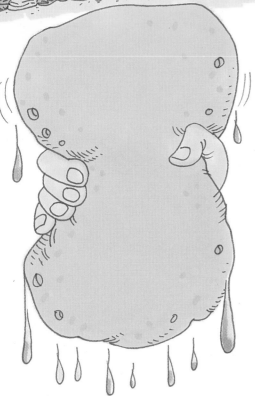

What are sponges made of?

Sponges are animals that live on the bottom of the ocean and never move. Some have beautiful shapes and fantastic colors. Sponges have a skeleton, cells that form chambers, and whip-like threads called *flagella* to capture tiny plants and animals for food.

How long does it take food to pass through my body?

About a day. Eat a burger today and it's gone tomorrow. Digestion—the breaking up of food into chemicals the body can use—begins with the saliva in the mouth, continues in the stomach, the small intestines, and then the large intestines. Your intestines, one long tube all coiled up, can be up to 30 feet long! They absorb nutrients and water from food, as it moves on down the line.

WHY CAN'T I BLOW BUBBLES WITH REGULAR GUM?

WHY CAN'T I BLOW BUBBLES WITH REGULAR GUM?

Trees have the secret ingredient. All gum contains gum base, sweeteners, and wood resin. Bubble gum has more wood resin, which provides the glue and the stretch. Without as much resin, regular gum isn't elastic enough to expand and hold the bubble you blow.

WHO WAS THE FIRST PERSON TO GET PIERCED EARS?

Earrings are ornaments of ancient Middle Eastern and East Indian civilizations. Both men and women wore them. Gold and silver, flowers and birds, pearls and gems were all worn on one ear or two depending on the style of the day. The Greeks even hung gold earrings on statues of goddesses.

When was the first car invented?

In 1770, Nicolas Cugnot, a French soldier, built a steam engine that travelled about three miles per hour. It was so big that this "self-propelled road vehicle" was impossible to steer. In 1862, J. J. Etienne Lenoir, of Paris, took his carriage with an internal combustion engine for its first ride: six miles in three hours at an average speed of two miles per hour.

I CAN BEAT IT IN A RACE EVERYTIME!!

HOW BIG WAS THE BIGGEST ICEBERG EVER?

Bigger than some countries! In 1956, an iceberg was sighted that was 208 miles long and 60 miles wide. That's about the size of Belgium. Only a small part of this ice monster was seen above water. Most icebergs hide nine-tenths of their size under the surface.

THAT'S A LOT OF ICE!

What causes twins?

"Identical" twins are born when one fertilized egg splits into two. They are the same sex and look alike. "Fraternal" twins are born when two eggs are fertilized. They can be a boy and a girl, or both the same sex. They usually resemble each other no more than any other siblings.

YOU LOOK LIKE ME!

YOU LOOK LIKE ME!

Why do plants turn to face the light?

Not to get a tan. Their leaves, which contain chlorophyll, create food in combination with light. So they must face the sun. They also have growth substances, which gather in the stem cells that do not face the light. This creates more growth on the shaded side than on the sunny side, which causes the plant to bend toward the light.

What is the Great Sphinx and the pyramids?

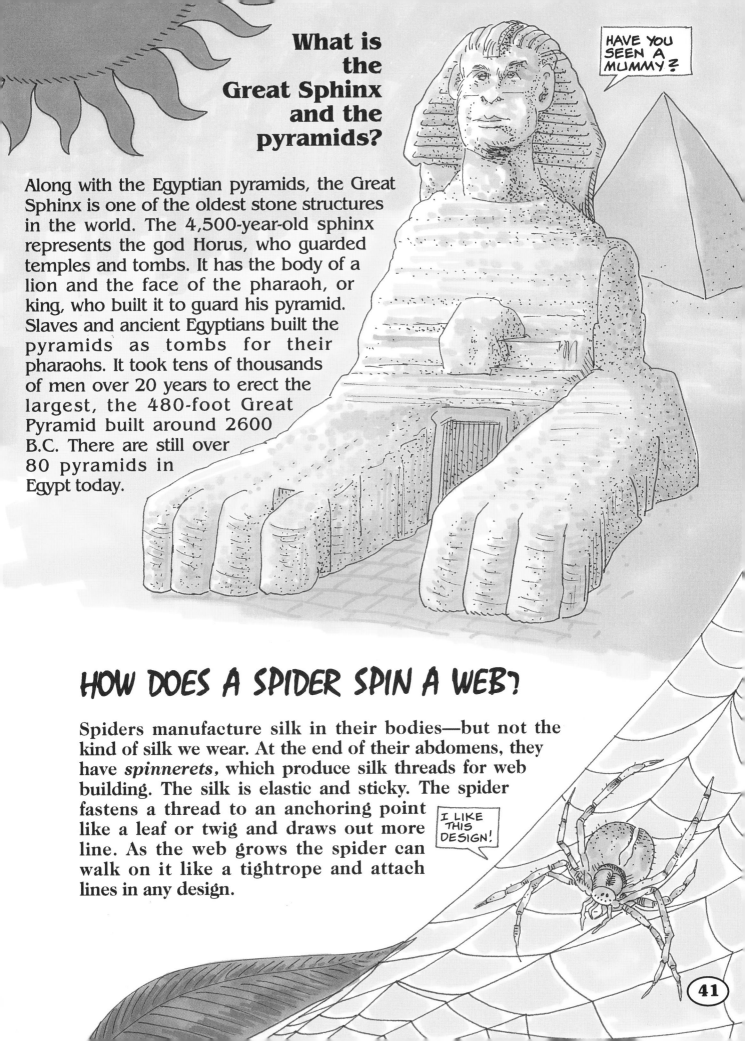

HAVE YOU SEEN A MUMMY?

Along with the Egyptian pyramids, the Great Sphinx is one of the oldest stone structures in the world. The 4,500-year-old sphinx represents the god Horus, who guarded temples and tombs. It has the body of a lion and the face of the pharaoh, or king, who built it to guard his pyramid. Slaves and ancient Egyptians built the pyramids as tombs for their pharaohs. It took tens of thousands of men over 20 years to erect the largest, the 480-foot Great Pyramid built around 2600 B.C. There are still over 80 pyramids in Egypt today.

HOW DOES A SPIDER SPIN A WEB?

Spiders manufacture silk in their bodies—but not the kind of silk we wear. At the end of their abdomens, they have *spinnerets*, which produce silk threads for web building. The silk is elastic and sticky. The spider fastens a thread to an anchoring point like a leaf or twig and draws out more line. As the web grows the spider can walk on it like a tightrope and attach lines in any design.

I LIKE THIS DESIGN!

Where was the world's largest birthday party?

In Buffalo, New York, on July 4, 1991, about 75,000 people sang "Happy Birthday" during a Friendship Festival that's held every year. Buffalo, not far from Canada, was celebrating the birthdays of both countries.

I HAVE SEEDS!

I DON'T!

I WASN'T INVITED TO THAT BIRTHDAY PARTY!

What's the difference between fruits and vegetables?

Seeds make the difference. Any fleshy part of a plant that grows from a flower is called its "fruit." If this part contains seeds, like an orange, an apple, a peach, or even a tomato, it's considered a fruit. If it has no seeds, like broccoli or lettuce or carrots, it's considered a vegetable.

Who was Queen Elizabeth I?

Queen Elizabeth I was England's queen from 1558 to 1603. She brought peace and prosperity to her devoted subjects, who called her "Good Queen Bess." She never married or shared her reign, and during her era— the Elizabethan Age—literature, drama, and music flourished. What a grand time it was!

Why is the sea salty?

There's salt in there. The salt content of an ocean is 3.5% by weight. The salt originates in rocks on the edges of the sea and in rivers and streams. Through the constant wetting and drying, the salt dissolves into the water and collects in the oceans.

I WASN'T INVITED TO THAT BIRTHDAY PARTY EITHER!

HOW DID PEOPLE CLEAN THEIR TEETH BEFORE TOOTHBRUSHES?

The natural way—twigs. People picked a good-tasting twig, chewed one end until it shredded, and used the "bristles." Or, they dipped their fingers in salt and rubbed their teeth. Three hundred years ago wooden-handled, hog-bristled toothbrushes were invented. In some places, they are still used.

... AND I SEE MY DENTIST TWICE A YEAR!

... AND I DON'T NEED BATTERIES!

How does a firefly make its light?

Only the firefly knows for sure. Scientists know that the light is *cold*, not hot like electric light. They know that both male and female fireflies flicker their lights to attract mates. And fireflies are not flies at all, but really beetles. But when it comes to how the firefly makes its light, scientists are still in the dark.

43

I SHOULD GO ON A DIET!

HOW MUCH DOES THE EARTH WEIGH?

6,600,000,000,000,000,000,000 tons. The Earth's mass, which is a different measurement than weight on scales, is 6.6 sextillion tons . . . and growing. Cosmic dust and meteorites add thousands of tons each year.

I CAN RUN FASTER THAN YOU!

SURE YOU CAN.

I REMEMBER WHEN EARTH WAS ONLY 6.5 SEXTILLION TONS!

WHAT'S THE DIFFERENCE BETWEEN A CAMEL AND A DROMEDARY?

One hump or two. There are two types of camels. Bactrian camels have two humps. The dromedary is a one-humped Arabian camel especially bred for riding and racing. These long-legged beasts can run about 10 miles an hour and travel as far as 100 miles a day.

WHAT IS THE OLDEST TREE IN THE WORLD?

A bristlecone pine on Mt. Wheeler in Nevada, was found to be 5,100 years old. The *inside* of a tree, not the outside, reveals its age. The number of rings seen on a tree stump or cut log tells the tree's age. Each ring is about a year's growth of wood cells.

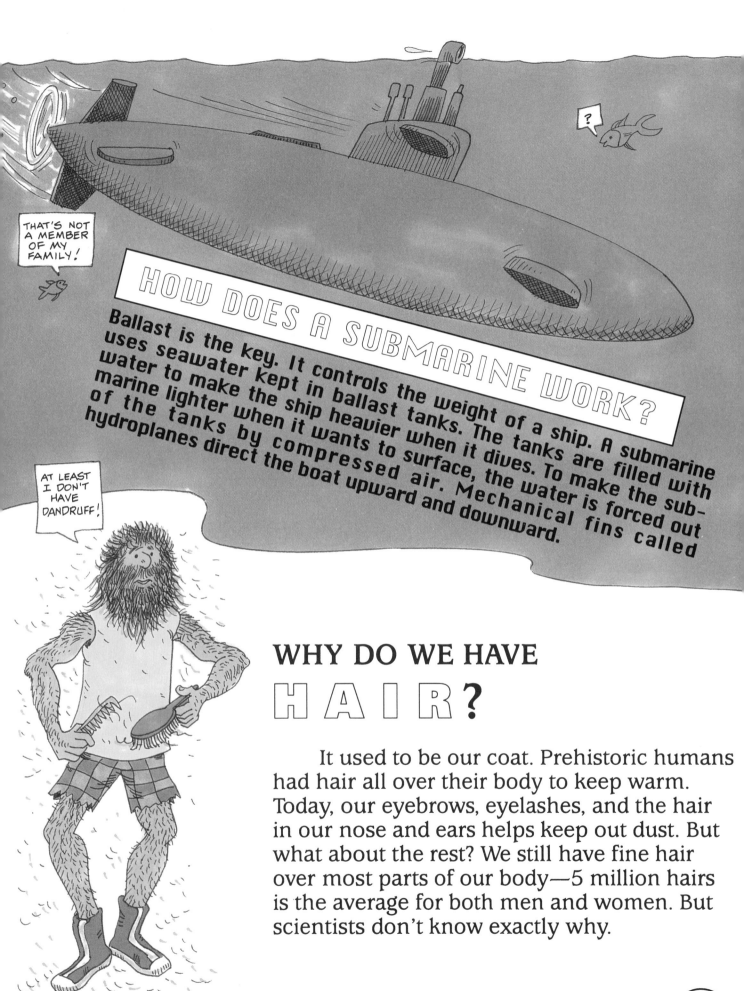

HOW DOES A SUBMARINE WORK?

Ballast is the key. It controls the weight of a ship. A submarine uses seawater kept in ballast tanks. The tanks are filled with water to make the ship heavier when it dives. To make the submarine lighter when it wants to surface, the water is forced out of the tanks by compressed air. Mechanical fins called hydroplanes direct the boat upward and downward.

WHY DO WE HAVE
H A I R?

It used to be our coat. Prehistoric humans had hair all over their body to keep warm. Today, our eyebrows, eyelashes, and the hair in our nose and ears helps keep out dust. But what about the rest? We still have fine hair over most parts of our body—5 million hairs is the average for both men and women. But scientists don't know exactly why.

WHAT MAKES SNOW?

First the temperature has to be below freezing. Then a drop of water vapor may form a crystal around a particle of dust in the atmosphere. Some crystals stick together and form snowflakes heavy enough to fall to Earth. All snowflakes are different. The individual crystals are the same, but no two combinations are identical.

How do bats see in the dark?

They "see" in the dark with sound. Bats make high-pitched sounds and then listen for the echoes, which bounce off whatever is ahead, such as a tree, a bird, or any object. From these echoes, they can tell direction and distance, and even the speed of a passing insect. This bat-brained system, called *echolocation*, lets them fly in total darkness.

THAT'S A LOT OF WATERING!

HOW MANY DIFFERENT PLANTS ARE THERE IN THE WORLD?

More than we know. About 350,000 species of plants are known, but new ones are constantly being discovered. Plants range from algae to orchids to giant sequoia trees, and they're a hardy bunch. They've been on the planet for 3 billion years. Animal life didn't join them until about 600 million years ago.

WHAT'S THE DIFFERENCE BETWEEN A WHITE EGG AND A BROWN EGG?

It's in the chicken. Some breeds of chickens lay white eggs and some brown. The eggs fry, scramble, boil, and taste the same.

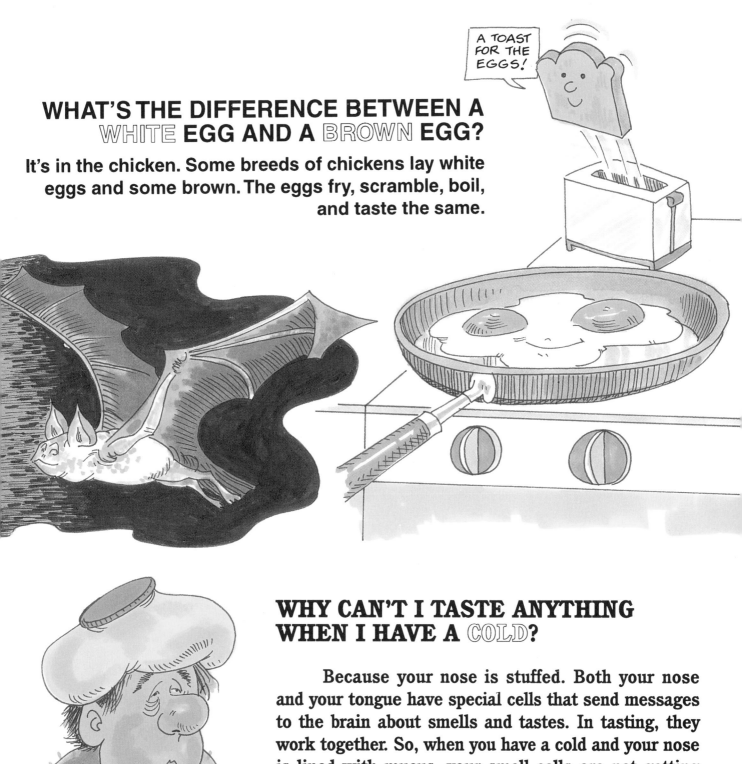

A TOAST FOR THE EGGS!

WHY CAN'T I TASTE ANYTHING WHEN I HAVE A COLD?

Because your nose is stuffed. Both your nose and your tongue have special cells that send messages to the brain about smells and tastes. In tasting, they work together. So, when you have a cold and your nose is lined with mucus, your smell cells are not getting the news that your tongue is tasting an orange. It's the pits.

47

WHAT'S THE MOST BEAUTIFUL PAINTING IN THE WORLD?

First, what's beautiful? Beauty in Los Angeles might not be the same in Timbuktu. Where you live changes how you feel about what's beautiful. And what *you* think is beautiful is probably different from a friend's idea of beauty. Beauty is personal. The painting considered to be one of the world's most beautiful, most famous, and most expensive (worth at least $100 million) is the "Mona Lisa." It was painted between 1503 and 1507 by Leonardo da Vinci.

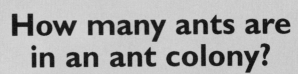

How many ants are in an ant colony?

That depends on the type of ant—and there are about 15,000 different kinds! But most ants are *social* insects that live in groups. Some colonies have only 10 ants and others have hundreds of thousands. Some nests are "hills," others are underground, and still others are built from leaves or found in wood. Wherever they live, ants will usually come out if you have a picnic.

WHY DO PEOPLE HAVE DIFFERENT COLOR SKINS?

The difference is only skin deep. Melanin is the substance in the skin that produces darker shades. Since melanin protects the skin from the sun, more cells are created when we are exposed to the sun, and the skin becomes darker. The theory is that, in ancient times, people who lived in sunny climates were darker skinned, and those that lived in colder areas were fair. People today have inherited the color of their ancestors.

WHAT WOULD HAPPEN IF ALL THE *ICE* IN THE WORLD MELTED?

I HAD BETTER LEARN TO SWIM!

Some people would have to move. The seas would rise about 20 feet and the coasts of continents would gradually disappear under water. Floods in America would claim major centers like New York and San Francisco. But don't panic. Scientists say the melting will happen, but not for thousands of years.

WHY DO MAGNETS ATTRACT?

Iron contains millions of tiny magnets called domains. Usually they are pointed in different directions and are not magnetized. A magnetized metal has all of its domains pointing in the same direction. All magnets have two poles, north and south, that pull iron and steel objects toward them, into their *magnetic field.* They only attract their opposites, north to south and south to north.

Why does hot water clean better than cold water?

It heats things up. Whatever's stuck on you dissolves better in heat. Soap grabs grease better in heat. And bacteria (tiny organisms that may carry disease) die in heat. Heat cleans things up.

I WAS WONDERING ABOUT THAT MYSELF!

HOW DO SNAKES MOVE IF THEY DON'T HAVE LEGS?

With a combination of muscles, scales, and an amazingly flexible spine. Snakes have belly scales, which grip the ground like tractor treads while their muscles pull their bodies forward. The spine is responsible for the snake's trademark curvy slither.

HOW IS PAPER MADE?

THIS IS GENUINE 100% PAPER !

It all starts with wood. Cut, ground up, mashed, watered, bleached, pressed, rolled out, and dried, wood becomes paper. Logs are ground up and combined with water and chemicals into a mixture called pulp. Shredded rags, glue, and coloring are added to make some papers. Then the pulp is dried and pressed into giant rolls.

What's my funny bone ?

It's not humorous . . . it's *humerus.* That's your funny-bone's real name. It connects with the bones of your fore-arm at the elbow, a place where there are a bunch of sensitive nerves. When you whack that spot, it's no joke.

WHAT'S SO FUNNY?

WHO WAS THE FIRST PERSON IN SPACE?

When Russian Cosmonaut Yuri Alekseyevich Gagarin took off on April 12, 1961, he was the first person to leave the Earth in a satellite. He was up there alone for 108 minutes. Before returning, he traveled 17,560 miles. Although unafraid, Yuri must have been in a hurry.

?

HI!

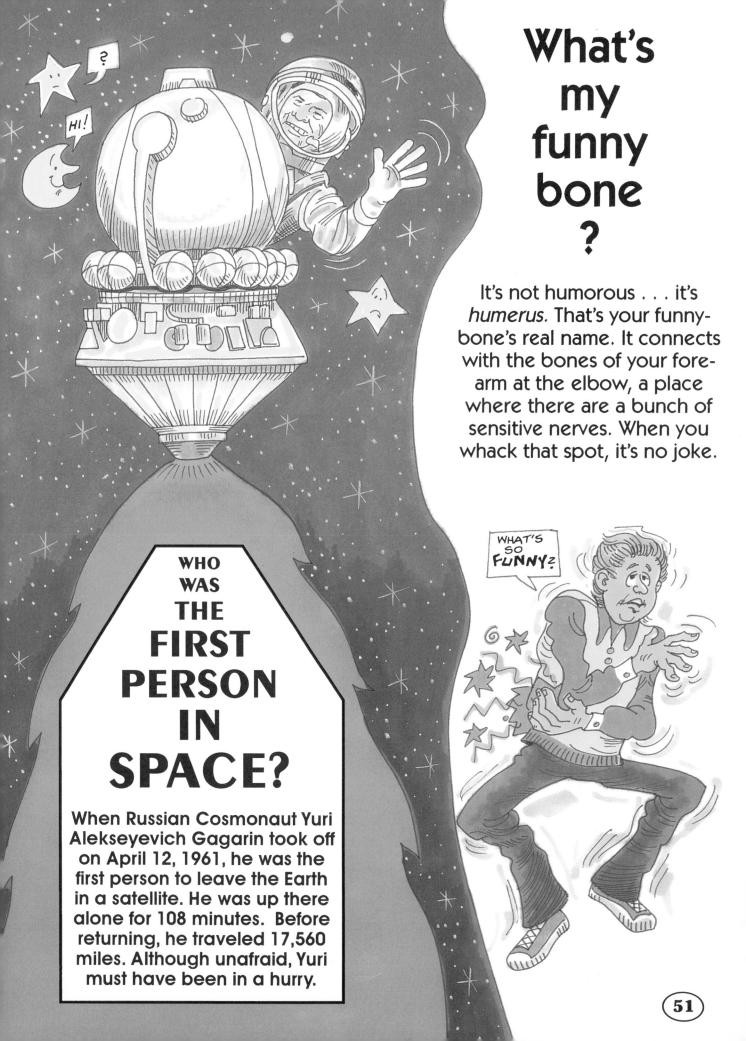

WHY DO I FEEL DIZZY WHEN I SPIN AROUND?

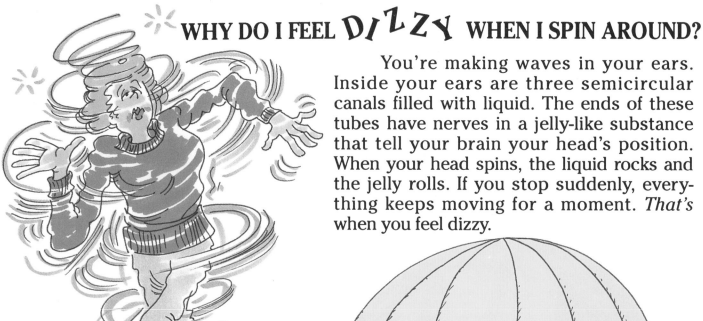

You're making waves in your ears. Inside your ears are three semicircular canals filled with liquid. The ends of these tubes have nerves in a jelly-like substance that tell your brain your head's position. When your head spins, the liquid rocks and the jelly rolls. If you stop suddenly, everything keeps moving for a moment. *That's* when you feel dizzy.

SHE'S MAKING ME DIZZY JUST WATCHING HER !!!

COME ON DOWN!

WHAT ANIMAL GATHERS IN THE LARGEST GROUP?

The seal. Each year about 1.5 million Alaskan fur seals gather on the Pribilof Islands off the coast of Alaska to breed. The result: 500,000 baby seals.

HOW DOES A PARACHUTE WORK?

Perfectly . . . or else! When brave men and women jump out of airplanes, they pull a cord, and a canopy, or parachute, opens above them. This umbrella-shaped cloth resists the air, counteracts the jumper's weight, and slows the fall. When the person hits the ground, the force is about the same as a long jump.

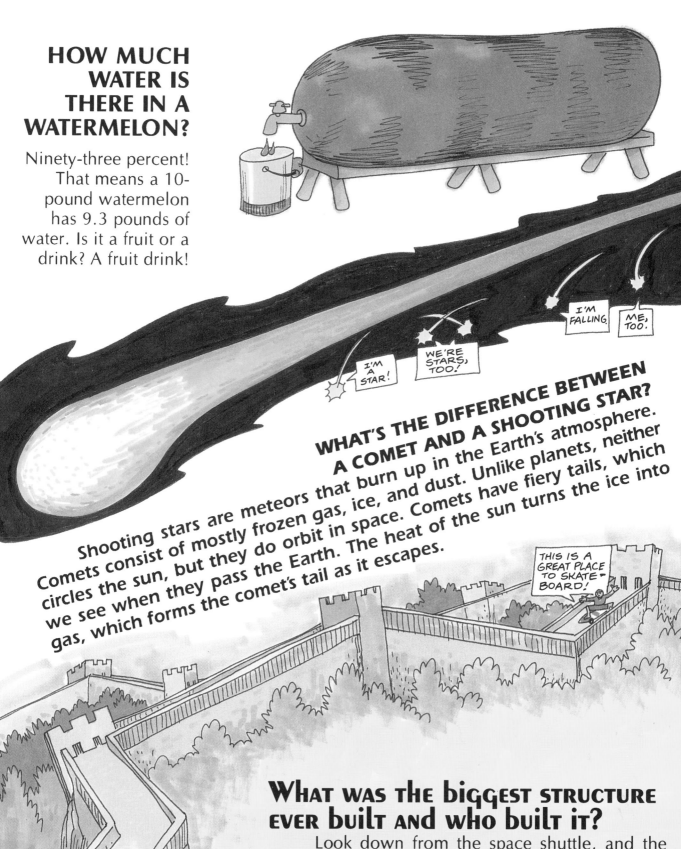

HOW MUCH WATER IS THERE IN A WATERMELON?

Ninety-three percent! That means a 10-pound watermelon has 9.3 pounds of water. Is it a fruit or a drink? A fruit drink!

WHAT'S THE DIFFERENCE BETWEEN A COMET AND A SHOOTING STAR?

Shooting stars are meteors that burn up in the Earth's atmosphere. Comets consist of mostly frozen gas, ice, and dust. Unlike planets, neither circles the sun, but they do orbit in space. Comets have fiery tails, which we see when they pass the Earth. The heat of the sun turns the ice into gas, which forms the comet's tail as it escapes.

WHAT WAS THE BIGGEST STRUCTURE EVER BUILT AND WHO BUILT IT?

Look down from the space shuttle, and the only human-made object you'll be able to see on Earth is the Great Wall of China. It's *that* big!

Built from 221 to 210 B.C., the wall is 2,150 miles long, with 1,780 miles of branches. In some places it's 39 feet high and 32 feet thick.

WHAT'S THE HOTTEST PLACE ON EARTH?

The hottest temperature ever recorded in the United States was 134°F in Death Valley, California, on July 10, 1913. It was not a cool summer. The thermometer hit 120°F for 43 days in a row. So, head for the shade, right? Not in Libya. On September 13, 1922, it was 136°F in that North African country—in the shade!

136°

THIS IS HOT!

0°

WHAT CAUSES A TORNADO?

Tornadoes form in storm clouds when masses of hot, humid air rise and begin to rotate. These rotating funnel clouds can extend down to the ground—and destroy everything in their path. At over 300 miles an hour, the funnel of a tornado is the fiercest wind on earth. But on the fringes, the wind can be gentler. In 1986, 12 Chinese children were sucked up by a tornado and dropped safely back down 12 miles away!

WHEN WAS THE CHOCOLATE BAR INVENTED?

In 1811. A chocolate drink was first brought to Europe from the Aztecs of Mexico in the 1500s. Three hundred years later, Francois-Louis Cailler of Switzerland manufactured the first chocolate in bars. How many things can you think of that have chocolate in them?

HOW DOES A PLANE STAY UP IN THE AIR?

SO, THAT'S HOW I FLY!

I DON'T HAVE WINGS!

Power and lift. Power comes from the engines. Lift comes from the wings, which are called airfoils. Airfoils are rounded on top, flat on the bottom, rounded on the front edge, and narrow at the back. Because of this shape, there is less air pressure on the top of the wing. The greater pressure under the wing pushes upward and keeps the plane from falling.

PLING!

OUCH!

Who Was King Arthur?

Arthur, an English king, is believed to have lived in the 6th century. No one is absolutely sure, but the legends about him are fantastic. They say that he was the only man to withdraw a magical sword from a stone. His Knights of the Roundtable included Sir Lancelot and Sir Galahad, the greatest soldiers in Europe. And he was supposedly handsome, courageous, and honest. It would be nice to know he really existed.

What's the star nearest to Earth?

Don't wait for dark to find it. Don't even take out your telescope. It's our very own daytime star, the sun, just 93 million miles away. The next closest star is Proxima Centauri, and it's 25 trillion miles from Earth.

WHAT IS ACID RAIN?

It's worse than bad weather. It's rain carrying chemical pollution. When industries burn coal and oil, sulfur and nitrogen rise into the air and dissolve in the atmosphere. When moisture forms, these chemicals become part of the water vapor that falls to the Earth as rain.

WHAT WAS THE WORLD'S FIRST DOG?

I KNEW HIM WELL!

A wolf-like creature. The wolf is a member of the scientific family Canidae, which developed about 20 million years ago. All dogs are related to this same ancestor and are part of the same family. But today, there are many different dogs because of *selective breeding*. People have bred dogs with certain characteristics until a whole line of descendants developed. Now the world has big dogs and small, long and short-haired, pointy and floppy-eared, making the tiny Chihuahua and huge St. Bernard strange, but true relatives.

I FLEW BEFORE THEM!

WHO INVENTED THE FIRST POWERED AIRCRAFT?

The Wright brothers, Orville and Wilbur. When their biplane (a plane with two sets of wings) rose above the ground at Kitty Hawk, North Carolina, in 1903, it was the first flight powered by an engine. First it bumped along, but on the fourth try, Wilbur was airborne for 59 seconds and flew 852 feet.

WHO WAS THE ORIGINAL DRACULA?

The main character in an 1897 novel by Englishman Bram Stoker. The author based his story "on a king Vlad Dracula," who lived in the 1400s in Wallachia, a part of Romania. He was better known as Vlad the Impaler for his nasty habit of sticking the bodies of his enemies on wooden stakes like a fence. He is said to have once impaled 20,000 people as a warning to the invading Turks.

I CAN'T STAY... I'M LATE FOR LUNCH!

FEET DO YOUR THING!!

I'D RATHER SEE THE MOVIE!!

HOW DO EARTHWORMS HELP THE GROUND?

They make the ground good for plants. Creeping and crawling, earthworms loosen up the soil so plants can wiggle their roots down. Also, by leaving waste behind, earthworms fertilize the ground for growing plants.

WHAT MAKES ICE CUBES CRACK WHEN YOU PUT THEM IN A DRINK?

I HEARD THAT!

A temperature clash. When the ice cube meets the liquid, its outside begins to warm up and expand. But its icy center remains frozen and unmoved. Pressure between the outer, expanding part of the cube and its frozen center builds up until...*snap!*—the ice cube cracks.

What kinds of instruments are in a symphony orchestra?

A ONE AND A TWO AND A THREE!

LET'S BEGIN.

WAIT FOR ME!

I'M READY!

The sound of a symphony is a mix of these: *percussion*, like the drums and cymbals; *brass*, like the trumpet and trombone; *woodwind*, like the flute and clarinet; and *strings*, like the violin and cello. Ninety to 120 players put it all together—and the result is sweet music.

LET'S EAT!

WHY DO MY CHEEKS GET RED IN THE WINTER?

It's warm blood coming to the rescue of your cold skin. In winter, you wear a hat, coat, and gloves but probably not a face mask. So your body, all on its own, sends more rosy, warm blood to the vessels under your cheeks. It protects your face from frostbite.

WHO ATE THE FIRST SANDWICH?

Someone who was too busy to use silverware. The honor goes to an Englishman named, of course, the Earl of Sandwich. In the 1700s, he put some food between two slices of bread, took a bite, and made history.

What do red giants, white dwarves, and black holes have in common?

Stardom. But not the Hollywood type. Having burned off most of their helium and hydrogen fuel, they are all stars nearing the end of their existence. The dying star first swells and becomes a red giant. Then its enormous gravitational force shrinks it down into a white dwarf, still giving off some light. But a black hole does not. If the star is massive enough, its gravitational pull is so strong that even light can't escape its surface.

WHY DO POLICE USE FINGERPRINTS TO TRACE PEOPLE?

Because the pattern of lines on the underside of your fingertips is yours alone. And they're the same for your whole life. The lines are called loops, whorls, and arches. No two people have the same pattern—even identical twins have different fingerprints.

Hot-Air Balloons

Want a quiet ride? Try a balloon. Hot-air balloons float when the air inside the balloon is heated. The heated air is lighter than the cool air outside, so the balloon rises toward the sky. Once released, the balloon will float as high as its weight allows. Then the pilot must throw weight off to go higher, or release air to descend.

HELICOPTERS

Want to hang out? Take a helicopter ride. Helicopters can hover, or hang in the air, over one spot. The *rotor blades* above the cockpit are the "wings" that provide the lift and the direction. At a certain speed, the blades hold the helicopter in one spot. At a faster speed, the blades will lift it higher. Tilted, they send the aircraft backward, forward, and sideways. A small rotor on the tail completes the balancing act.

HAVE A NICE FLIGHT!

JET PLANE

Want to travel fast? Take a jet plane. The jet engine is called a turbofan. Fans at the front of the engine suck air into a compression chamber, where it is mixed with fuel and fired. The heated, high-pressure air and the exhaust gases rush out the back of the engine and thrust the plane forward. The first jet plane took off in 1947.

Airship

Want to travel light? Fly by airship. An airship is a cabin carried by a huge balloon filled with *helium*, a gas seven times lighter than air. The rising or *upthrust* of this balloon is so powerful that it can carry an engine, along with cabin and passengers. Small propellers and a rudder do the steering. Early airships carried as many as 200 people, but today's are usually the smaller variety—the blimp.

ROCKET

Want to blast off? Ride a rocket. A rocket is a heat engine with solid or liquid fuel, called a *propellant*. The basic principle of a rocket is the same as a firecracker. A highly flammable substance is packed into a chamber and fired. The hot gases that result stream out from the base and drive the rocket upward. It takes five huge rockets to shoot a space shuttle into orbit.

THAT'S ME!

Who was Leonardo da Vinci?

WHAT'S FOR LUNCH?

A genius. Leonardo (1452-1519) lived during the Italian Renaissance, a great artistic period. He is famous as a painter, and his work, the *Mona Lisa* is one of the most valuable paintings in the world. But he was also a scientist, inventor, engineer, architect, and designer. He made brilliant observations that paved the way for future scientists and inventors.

HOW DO PLANTS EAT?

They make food. They cook up sugars using the process of *photosynthesis*, which combines sunlight, carbon dioxide, and water from the soil. *Chlorophyll*, a green pigment which captures the sun's energy, makes this possible. Some plants that can't get what they need from the soil dine on insects. They capture them with sticky leaves—or petals that snap together like jaws.

I'M THE DRUMMER BOY.

WHY DO SOLDIERS SALUTE?

It's a military rule. A salute is a sign of respect to a person of higher rank. Bowing or kneeling to royalty or officers has gone on throughout history. A hand-to-the-forehead salute probably comes from taking off a hat as a gesture of respect—which may have come from the way knights removed their helmets when speaking to nobles.

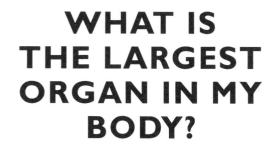

I-I-I'M C-C-COLD!

WHAT IS THE LARGEST ORGAN IN MY BODY?

THE LAYER THAT PROTECTS ALL OF YOU— YOUR SKIN. AN ADULT MAN HAS ABOUT 20 SQUARE FEET OF SKIN, A WOMAN, 17 SQUARE FEET. (THAT'S IF IT WERE TAKEN OFF AND LAID OUT TO MEASURE.) SKIN FLAKES OFF ALL THE TIME. IT TAKES ABOUT A MONTH FOR NEW TISSUE TO REPLACE OLD.

When was the first zipper zipped?

In 1893, but it didn't stay closed for long. This first version, for boots and shoes, didn't work well. In 1913, Gideon Sundback invented a zipper that stayed zipped. Nobody cared until World War I in 1917, when zippers began appearing on military uniforms. Still, it wasn't until 1938 that the zipper replaced the buttons on men's pants.

WHAT IS THE "GREENHOUSE EFFECT?"

It's hot stuff. Scientists have noticed that the Earth's atmosphere is gradually getting warmer. Carbon dioxide gas, which is given off by the burning of fossil fuels like coal, traps the sun's heat and warms the Earth. The gas absorbs the heat of both the sun and the Earth, just as heat is absorbed by the glass of a greenhouse for plants.

Who invented the ice-cream cone?

Italo Marcioni. He got a patent for a special cone mold in 1896. But ice cream didn't really meet cone in a big way until 1904 at the St. Louis Fair. An ice-cream vendor was next to a waffle maker. One rolled up a waffle—the other put ice cream in it. The rest is history.

What makes whirlpools whirl?

Water that flows in a certain direction is called a current. When two currents collide, the force forms a swirl of water. Currents whipped by the wind, pulled by the tides, and interrupted by rocks can also form whirlpools. Some are powerful enough to suck down whatever gets caught in the middle.

GULP!

HOW DO THE HOLES GET INTO SWISS CHEESE?

Bacteria puts them there. Cheese is a food whose flavor and texture is created by bacteria. The holes in Swiss cheese are made by "bubbles" of gas given off by its busy builders.

WHAT IS THE WORLD'S MOST POPULATED CITY?

Tokyo, Japan, and it's growing. Tokyo's metropolitan area had a population of about 26 million people in 1994 and is expected to reach 28 million people by the year 2000.

HOW DOES A LIGHT BULB LIGHT UP?

With a de*light*ful combination of electricity, metal, heat, and gas. Inside a bulb is a thin filament (wire) of tungsten, a metal with a very high melting point. That means it can take a lot of heat without melting. Electrical current heats the filament (as high as 4,500 degrees!) so that it glows with light. The bulb is airtight and filled with an inactive gas called argon, which keeps oxygen out and helps the bulb last longer.

WHAT ARE ROBOTS USED FOR?

Robots are good at doing the same task over and over again, exactly the same way. All robots are machines that have computer instructions built in. They paint cars. They lift heavy loads. They enter radioactive or hot areas too dangerous for humans. Some are simply arms and a gripper, with humans controlling them from a distance.

WHAT IS

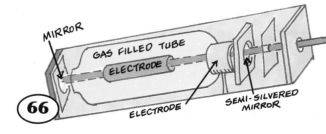

MIRROR

GAS FILLED TUBE

ELECTRODE

ELECTRODE

SEMI-SILVERED MIRROR

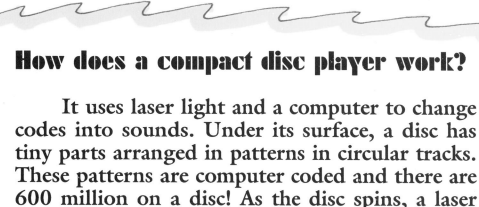

How does a compact disc player work?

It uses laser light and a computer to change codes into sounds. Under its surface, a disc has tiny parts arranged in patterns in circular tracks. These patterns are computer coded and there are 600 million on a disc! As the disc spins, a laser light reads the patterns, sending electrical signals to a computer. The player's computer has a memory of all the possible signals, and turns the code into sounds.

WHAT ARE
X RAYS?

Rays of energy similar to light rays. But unlike light, they travel *through* you. When an X ray is taken, the rays penetrate your body and strike a piece of photographic film. The result is a shadow picture of your insides. Denser parts, like bones, are brighter because they absorb X rays. Fleshy parts are dimmer because the rays pass through them.

A LASER?

A very intense beam of light. Lasers are created when the molecules of gases, liquids, or solids are so excited by electricity that they burst into a single, concentrated, powerful stream of light. Some cut through steel or drill holes in diamonds. Others perform everyday tasks. They play audio discs and read the bar codes on groceries.

IS THERE LIFE ON OTHER PLANETS?

Not likely in our solar sytem. Certainly no creatures with melon heads and almond eyes. No little green men. The other planets don't have atmospheres that could support life as we know it on Earth. And their temperatures are extreme—too hot or too cold. We know the moon has no life because we've been there. And space probes have found no life on Mars. But there may be planets similar to Earth revolving around some of the billions and billions of stars in outer space.

WHO CREATED THE ALPHABET?

For thousands of years people drew pictures, creating a symbol—like a drawing of the sun—to stand for an object or an idea. The ancient Egyptians and other Middle Eastern peoples were the first to communicate this way. That was about 5,000 years ago. About 3,000 years ago, the Greeks had a complete alphabet. The Greek alphabet was further changed by the Romans in the first century A.D. It's the Roman alphabet that English is based on. You can see the history in the word "alphabet." It comes from the first two letters of the Greek alphabet, alpha and beta.

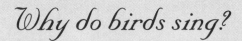

Why do birds sing?

Birds raise their voices to send messages. Mostly males do it. They call out to attract mates or to send a note to other males: "I'm here. Back off!" But this feathered language is a sweet sound. To human ears, it sounds like singing.

TO OLYMPICS

WANT TO RACE?

WHERE WERE THE FIRST OLYMPICS HELD?

Olympia, Greece. The ancient Greek Olympics, held over 2,000 years ago, are the inspiration for today's games. The Greeks ended their games in 393 B.C., and it wasn't until 1896 that the games began again as an international event. The world has missed only three dates, 1916, 1940, and 1944 because of the two world wars.

WHY ARE SO MANY PEOPLE RIGHT-HANDED?

Your brain decides. But there are still some things about the brain that scientists don't know—and this is one of them. Nine out of ten people are right-handed. Nobody knows why.

How can I get SUNBURNED on a cloudy day?

If it's daytime, the sun is out whether we can see it or not. The sun's energy reaches us mostly as heat and light, but 6% is ultraviolet radiation (UVR), which causes sunburn. Clouds and pollution block some UVR, but the sun's rays are so strong that dangerous amounts still reach us.

How do crickets make their sound?

They wing it. Crickets, like most insects, have no vocal chords. But they do have some things to say, like "Hello," or "Here I am." Crickets make a noise by rubbing the hard, ridged tips of their wings together. That's cricket communication, but it's music to *our* ears.

I DON'T PLAY CRICKET.

Why do the continents look as though they fit together like a jigsaw puzzle?

One theory is that the Earth was once a huge single land mass that broke up. Over millions of years, pieces slowly drifted apart and became the continents as we know them today. The continents and the oceans have gigantic plates beneath them that move very slowly. So the positions of the continents are always changing ever so slightly.

IT FITS!

NORTH AMERICA
EUROPE
ASIA
AFRICA
SOUTH AMERICA
AUSTRALIA
ANTARCTICA

Who invented ROCK 'N' ROLL?

It was born in the 1950s. It grew from rhythm and blues music played by African-American artists like Chuck Berry, Little Richard, and others. Combined with gospel, folk, and country and western music, it came together in a new sound. Elvis Presley sold millions of rock 'n' roll records and became known as the "King of Rock 'n' Roll." When the Beatles brought their music from England in the 1960s, rock 'n' roll was here to stay.

I DIDN'T KNOW THAT!

WHAT IS A MUMMY?

It's not necessarily what most people think of—an Egyptian corpse wrapped in cloth. When bacteria and fungi cannot grow in a dead body, it becomes *mummified*. A mummy still has some of the body's soft tissues (skin, muscles, or organs). Some mummies were made by *embalming*, which is any process used to preserve a dead body. Ancient Egyptians did this with linen and tree resin (sap) because they believed in preparing the body for life after death. However, humans and animals have been found naturally mummified all over the world, usually in very dry or very cold places.

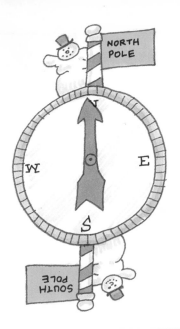

Why does a compass always point North?

THERE'S AN INVISIBLE, BUT NOT MYSTERIOUS, FORCE AT WORK. THE NEEDLE ON A COMPASS IS A THIN, FREELY SWINGING MAGNET. THE EARTH IS ALSO A GIANT MAGNET, WITH ITS NORTH AND SOUTH POLES NEAR THE NORTH AND SOUTH POLES ON THE MAP. THE NORTH POLE OF THE EARTH'S MAGNETIC FIELD ATTRACTS THE NORTH POLE OF THE NEEDLE, CAUSING IT TO POINT NORTH.

WHY DOES SOME SPOILED FOOD TURN GREEN?

It's the dreaded mold. Mold is all around us in the air and in the ground. It's a kind of fungus that grows in moist places, on food left out on the counter, and even on forgotten food in the back of the refrigerator. The tiny bits of mold grow into a large, green colony.

HOW OLD IS THE EARTH?

Very old—about 4.6 billion years. Primitive forms of life, like algae and bacteria, began to appear about a billion years later, when the planet developed the water and oxygen necessary to support living things. Fossils exist that show primitive life forms from 3.5 million years ago.

WHY DO I GET A SCAB WHEN I GET A CUT?

NICE MASK!

WHY DO PEOPLE DRESS IN COSTUMES ON HALLOWEEN?

To scare away the ghosts. In ancient times, the Celtic peoples of England prepared themselves for the dark days of winter with a festival. They lit bonfires and sacrificed animals. They expected evil spirits to be roaming about. To hide from them, they dressed up in costumes.

I'M NOT WEARING A MASK!

Who was Hans Christian Andersen?

HE WROTE ABOUT ME.

The man who wrote "The Ugly Duckling," "The Emperor's New Clothes," "The Princess and the Pea," and 165 other fairy tales. He was Danish, wrote during the 1800s, and told stories that still make us laugh and sigh today.

It's a natural bandage. Healthy blood cells come to the rescue of those torn by a cut. They thicken and clot, and add chemicals and other substances, which dry, shrink, and harden the cut cells. Then they become a scab—a seal that keeps blood in and germs out.

Because clouds are masses of water droplets and ice crystals. Sometimes shadows make clouds look gray. But usually, the more dense the water within a cloud, the grayer it is—and the sooner the rain.

IT'S NOT RAINING!

IT'S RAINING!

CAN ALL BIRDS FLY?

WHY SHOULD I FLY? I'M NOT GOING ANYWHERE!

Not big birds. Not the penguin, nor the ostrich. The shape of giant birds like the ostrich, the South American rhea, and the Australian emu keeps them from flying, as much as their weight does. Small birds have enormous breast muscles relative to the rest of their streamlined bodies that enable them to flap their wings. Big birds don't.

WHERE IS THE WORLD'S BIGGEST CAVE?

Mammoth Cave National Park in Kentucky has many interconnected cave passages. Together, they form a cave system whose overall length has been mapped at 348 miles.

WHAT IS A TIDAL WAVE?

A skyscraper of a wave. The Japanese call it *tsunami* (su-NAM-ee) for giant wave. A tsunami is created by an earthquake or a volcanic eruption—a violent shake-up of the ocean's floor. These waves, moving at up to 500 miles an hour, gain height and hit hard. In 1883, a tsunami in Indonesia killed 36,000 people after a fierce volcanic explosion off the island of Krakatoa.

THAT'S *FAST!*

If the Earth is *moving,* why can't we feel it?

I DON'T FEEL A THING!

MAYBE THAT'S WHY I ACT DIZZY!!

Gravity keeps our feet on the ground. We move along with the Earth's surface, as does the air around us, so we don't feel it as the Earth spins—at a speed of about 66,000 miles per hour!

What's the difference between an alligator

I'M HUNGRY!

and a crocodile?

SO AM I!

An alligator has a broader, rounder snout. A crocodile's snout is thinner and pointier. When a crocodile closes its mouth, the larger teeth on its bottom jaw rest in spaces on the **outside** of its upper jaw. In an alligator's mouth, they rest on the **inside** of the jaw.

HOW DO MOLES LIVE UNDER-GROUND?

FOR RENT

THEY CONSTANTLY DIG TUNNELS WITH THEIR STRONG FRONT CLAWS SEARCHING FOR TASTY WORMS AND GRUBS TO EAT. THE TUNNELS ALSO CONNECT THEM TO UNDERGROUND NESTS AND RESTING PLACES. THEIR MOLEHILLS, THE EXCESS EARTH FROM ALL THAT DIGGING, HAVE RUINED MANY A LAWN.

How and why do chameleons change color?

It's hide-and-seek in the animal world every day. Some animals hide while others seek to eat them. The chameleon has a natural ability to hide by changing its colors to match its surroundings. If it stays long enough in one spot, its color cells will change to blend in with the background. They also change color when it's too hot or cold, or if they feel threatened.

I SEE YOU!!

Where is the world's highest waterfall?

Venezuela. A good place for visiting, but not canoeing. Angel Falls (*Salto Angel*) on the Carrao River plunges 3,212 feet. Hills that high are called mountains.

Why can I see myself in a mirror?

Everything you see comes from light rays that bounce off objects and bounce back to your eyes. A mirror is glass with a shiny chemical coating on the back. When you stand in front of a mirror, light rays bounce off your body onto the mirror's coating. Then the rays reflect, or bounce back, to your eyes. What you are is what you see—it's your reflection.

WHAT ARE SUNSPOTS?

They're cool. Sunspots are places on the surface of the sun caused by changes in the sun's magnetic field. The surface temperature of the sun is about 10,000°Fahrenheit. Sunspots are about 3,600 degrees cooler. But cool on the sun is still hot, hot, hot.

IT'S HOT HERE!

HOW MUCH WOULD I WEIGH ON THE MOON?

If you weighed 100 pounds on Earth, you would weigh only 16.6 pounds on the moon. The reason is gravity, not some space-craze diet! The moon's gravity is one-sixth that of the Earth's. So your body mass is not pulled down so "heavily." Of course, your mass, height, and shape stay the same on the moon—only the numbers on a scale would change.

I'M GOING TO MOVE TO THE MOON!

WHERE IS THE LARGEST LIBRARY?

I THINK I TOOK OUT TOO MANY BOOKS!

The United States Library of Congress in Washington, DC. Know what you want before you go there, because it contains over 100 million items. And don't get lost in the shelves—there are 575 miles of them. The first modern public library in the United States was in New Hampshire in 1833, and it had 700 books. The largest public library today is in Chicago, and it's stacked with 11.4 million books.

WHAT MAKES A VOLCANO ERUPT?

A volcano erupting is a...**BLAST!** that comes from below. Volcanoes are located in places where plates are shifting beneath the Earth's crust. In such spots, hot liquid rock (magma) and gases are trying to escape. Pressure from these elements builds up until . . . **WHOOSH!** . . . they shoot up the center of a volcano. Fire, smoke, and ashes leap into the sky and lava pours down the sides of the volcano.

I'M BLOWING MY TOP!

I'D HAVE MY OWN TV SERIES ... IF TV HAD BEEN INVENTED!

WHEN WAS THE FIRST PLAY PERFORMED?

A *long* time ago—around 500 B.C. The first dramatists were the Greeks. They wrote and performed tragedies—serious plays—as well as comedies to make people laugh. Some plays have survived and are still performed today! The ancient Greek plays are considered to be among the great literature of the world.

FUNNY!

SAD!

79

How does the ice in a skating rink keep from MELTING?

Watch your toes, the floor is freezing. Beneath the ice is a concrete floor with pipes that are filled with a freezing solution. An Olympic rink may have up to 11 miles of these chilling pipes. So the weather above doesn't affect the ice as much as the temperature below.

WHO WAS KING TUT?

Tutankhamen (toot-ang-KAH-men) was his name, and he has been called the "boy king" of Egypt. Tut became king in 1361 B.C. when he was only nine years old. He died when he was about 19. His tomb and its fabulous riches weren't discovered until 1922—3,000 years after he was buried. He was found in a coffin made from 2,500 pounds of gold!

WHAT MAKES RAINBOWS APPEAR?

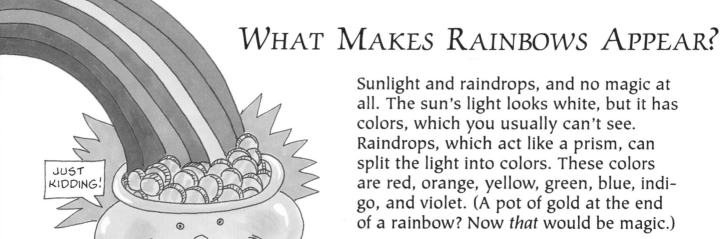

Sunlight and raindrops, and no magic at all. The sun's light looks white, but it has colors, which you usually can't see. Raindrops, which act like a prism, can split the light into colors. These colors are red, orange, yellow, green, blue, indigo, and violet. (A pot of gold at the end of a rainbow? Now *that* would be magic.)

HOW DOES AN ELECTRIC EEL MAKE ELECTRICITY?

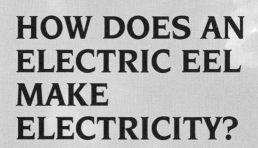

Body batteries. Electric eels, and other fish like the torpedo ray and some catfish, have thousands of linked natural battery cells in a coat of muscle tissue. A six-foot-long South American electric eel can generate a 500-volt zap of electricity—enough to light up a dozen bulbs.

WHAT IS CORAL?

A coral *polyp* is a tiny ocean animal with a skeleton on the outside and a soft body inside. When the body dies, the skeleton remains. Some corals live in large colonies. Their skeletons, millions and millions of them, form *reefs*, a giant wall of coral in the sea not far from shore. Corals can be shaped like flowers, fans, fingers, or even giant brains.

HOW DO FISH BREATHE?

Fish need oxygen just like we do. But we get it from air, and they get it from water. We use our lungs. They use their gills. Fish suck in water and pass it over their gills, which act as filters. The gills take oxygen from the water and pass it on to the blood vessels.

HOW DOES A COMPUTER THINK?

It doesn't. Computers *operate*. They do amazing things, but not without instructions. A computer has four basic units: memory, input, central processing, and output. The **memory** holds programs that tell the computer how to perform different tasks (play games, process words, add numbers, etc.). The **input** unit (keyboard) provides the information (data) that the program will work on. The **processing unit** uses the data to follow the program and work out results. The **output** unit displays the results—on a screen or through a printer.

I DON'T WRITE LETTERS!

EVERYONE WRITES LETTERS!

WHEN WAS THE FIRST POSTAGE STAMP USED?

In 1840 in Great Britain. Queen Victoria's picture was printed on over 60 million stamps called "Penny Blacks." George Washington and Benjamin Franklin were given the same honor in the United States seven years later. Many people collect stamps. One of the first British Penny Blacks was sold in 1991 for over $2 million.

WHERE DOES **CHOCOLATE** COME FROM?

Most people don't care as long as they can eat it, chew it, drink it, or let it melt in their mouths. The cocoa tree and its bean are the source of chocolate. When the beans are melted down, they become liquid cocoa. **DO NOT** drink it. It's so bitter it puckers up your mouth. Lots of sugar is added before it becomes chocolate.

How can a scientist tell how old a fossil is?

Radioactivity—it goes on and on. Mineralized fossils give off small amounts of nuclear radioactivity. The radioactivity slowly decreases over thousands and thousands of years. So scientists can take a bone, measure the changes in radioactivity, and tell how long ago the plant or animal lived.

Why do leaves turn colors in the fall?

For the tree's survival. Trees must shed their leaves to conserve water during the winter. So a film forms where the leaf joins the tree, cutting off food. That's when the colors change. Chlorophyll, which makes the leaf green, begins to break down. All the other colors—yellow, red, gold, and purple—which were hidden by the green, begin to show.

WHY DOES THE MOON CHANGE SHAPE IN THE SKY?

It doesn't. Only what we *see* changes. The moon circles the entire Earth about once every month. The moon reflects the sun's light. As it travels, we see the whole moon or parts of it, depending on where we are on Earth. These are the moon's *phases*, from a curved sliver to a full moon and back again.

Why do roosters crow in the morning?

It's their mating call. Roosters crow to attract females. They learned to crow when the light was dim—early morning and just before dark so their enemies were less likely to see them.

Who was Sitting Bull?

A fierce Native American leader, who tried to keep settlers from taking the land of his people, the Sioux. In 1876, Sitting Bull led nearly 2,000 warriors in one of the greatest defeats of American troops—the Battle of Little Bighorn.

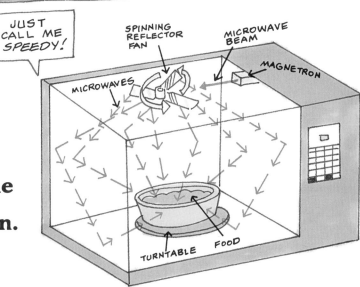

HOW DOES A MICROWAVE OVEN WORK?

Fast. In a microwave oven, a strong electrical current is changed into tiny *micro* waves. These radiate inside the oven, pass right through the food, bounce off the walls, and zip through the food again. The inside and outside are cooked all at once. In a regular oven, heat waves hit the outside of food and slowly cook inward.

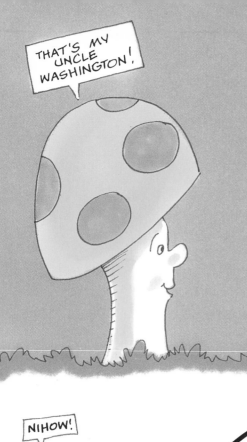

THAT'S MY UNCLE WASHINGTON!

WHAT IS THE WORLD'S LARGEST LIVING ORGANISM?

A mushroom. You just can't see it. Most of a mushroom plant is underground. The edible part sticks up. (Some are poisonous. *Never* pick and eat a mushroom.) One of the world's largest, called a honey or shoestring fungus, covers 1,500 acres in a Washington State forest. Scientists believe it's 500 to 1,000 years old!

How many languages are there in the world?

About 3,000. And English has the most words. Start increasing your vocabulary because there are over 600,000 words in English plus another 400,000 technical terms. But don't worry, no one knows them all. Even Shakespeare only used about 33,000.

NIHOW! — CHINA
GOED DAG! — DUTCH
BON JOUR! — FRANCE
GUTEN TAG! — GERMANY
YAISOU! — GREEK
SHALOM! — HEBREW
BON GIORNO! — ITALY
OHIO! — JAPAN
GOD MORGEN! — NORWAY
DUBRY DEN! — POLISH
WE ALL SAY HELLO! — U.S.A.
JAMBO! — SWAHILI
BUENOS DIAS! — SPANISH
ZDRASTVOUKEE! — RUSSIAN
BOM DIA! — PORTUGUESE

WHY DOES A GIRAFFE HAVE SUCH A **LONG** NECK?

Animal traits develop over thousands of years. The ones that last are characteristics that help them eat well and avoid enemies. A long neck gives the giraffe two important advantages. It can eat the leaves on the tops of trees that other animals can't reach. And it can see enemies coming from a long way off.

I COULD PLAY PRO BASKETBALL!

Why do I need sleep?

Get up—Go to school—Eat—Run around—Think—Throw a ball. Your body is working all day long. Waste builds up and slows down your systems. It makes you feel tired. Sleep is the time when your body cleans up, repairs, and relaxes. You must sleep. How much? Only your body knows.

87

YUM!

WHEN DID PEOPLE START EATING WITH KNIVES AND FORKS?

Knives were the first tool for killing *and* eating. During dinner, people cut their food with a knife and ate it with their hands. Forks came into use in Italy in the 1500s when fancy-dressed people found their lacy sleeves trailing in the mashed potatoes. In 1699, the king of France started the tradition of using knives with rounded ends.

WHO BUILT THE TAJ MAHAL AND WHY?

The magnificent Taj Mahal in northern India is a mausoleum, or tomb, built by the emperor Shah Jahan in memory of his wife. The mausoleum gets its name from *her* name, Mumtaz Mahal, which means "ornament of the palace." Twenty thousand men worked for over 20 years to build the complex, which includes several buildings, a reflecting pool, and a walled garden. The square tomb (186 feet on each side) has white marble walls, decorated with semiprecious stones, and is topped by five marble domes. The building was completed in 1648. Shah Jahan is also buried there.

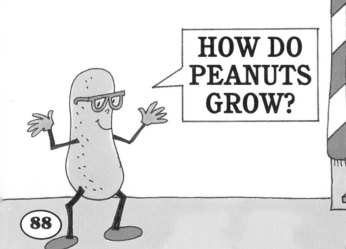

HOW DO PEANUTS GROW?

Upside down. "Nuts" are really the seeds of the plant they come from. Most plants grow up toward the sun. But not the nutty peanut plant. Its seed pods grow downward and bury themselves in the soil. Then the peanut ripens underground.

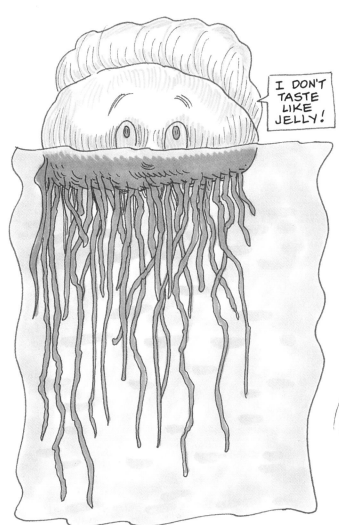

I DON'T TASTE LIKE JELLY!

WHAT ARE JELLYFISH?

They're not really fish, because they don't have backbones. Jellyfish are undersea creatures with tentacles and a jelly-like body shaped like an upside down cup. The sting you feel in the water is the poison a jellyfish releases to catch prey. The Portuguese man-of-war has tentacles that can be more than 100 feet long. It can produce very painful stings if touched by a human.

WHY DO MY MUSCLES ACHE WHEN I EXERCISE A LOT?

Bend your elbow, clench your fist, and make a muscle in your arm. Feel the muscle get rounder and firmer? Now let go. Feel it stretch and relax? When you *contract* and *relax* a muscle, the tissues produce lactic acid. That creates the achy, tired feeling you get. Rest, and you're ready to go again.

OOOPS!

HOW DO FIREWORKS WORK?

All that dazzle, flash, and sparkle is chemistry in motion. A firecracker is a two-staged event set off by gunpowder, chemicals, and a fuse. Light a firecracker and the gunpowder sends it flying. Then the fuse ignites the chemicals—and pow—strontium burns red; barium, green; copper, blue; and sodium, yellow. But remember, all that beauty is dangerous. Keep your hands *off!*

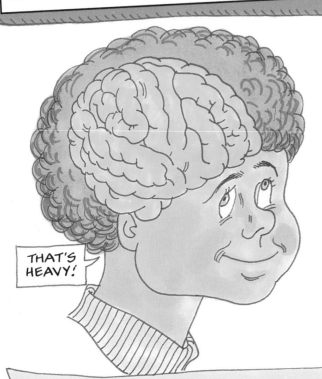

THAT'S HEAVY!

HOW MUCH DOES MY BRAIN WEIGH?

About 2% of your body weight. That's two pounds if you weigh 100. But the brain needs about ten times more of your body's resources— 20% of the oxygen you breathe, 20% of the calories in the food you eat, and 15% of the blood you have. Your busy brain needs lots of fuel to keep you going.

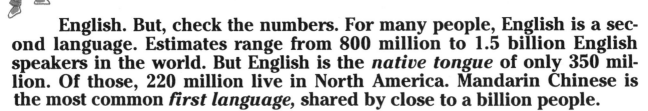

WHICH LANGUAGE IS SPOKEN BY THE MOST PEOPLE IN THE WORLD?

English. But, check the numbers. For many people, English is a second language. Estimates range from 800 million to 1.5 billion English speakers in the world. But English is the *native tongue* of only 350 million. Of those, 220 million live in North America. Mandarin Chinese is the most common *first language,* shared by close to a billion people.

THANK YOU!

SHIEH-SHIEH!

WHY DO MANY FLOCKS OF BIRDS FLY IN "V" FORMATION?

For the same reason one bicyclist rides right behind another. The first person breaks through the wind, lowering the wind resistance for the second person. In the case of birds, the leader's flapping wings create swirling air. The weaker birds behind catch a ride on these currents.

WHO FIRST STARTED USING MAKEUP?

Japanese actors, African dancers, Egyptian princesses, and Roman empresses. Makeup has been around since ancient times. Over two thousand years ago Cleopatra, the queen of Egypt, blackened her upper eyelids and lashes and put dark green color under her eyes. Red was the color of choice for cheeks and lips in Rome. What's new today? Not much—just more brands and colors to choose from.

"I DO IT!"

WHY DO THE TIDES RISE AND FALL?

High and low tides are the work of the moon. The moon's gravity pulls at the Earth's waters, raising and lowering them. When the moon and the sun are on the same side of the Earth, they both pull at the water. These tides are the highest. They're called "Spring" tides, even when they occur in Fall, Summer, or Winter.

"HI, GUYS!"

"IT'S HIGH TIDE!"

"IT'S LOW TIDE!"

HOW MANY BONES ARE IN MY BODY?

Adults have 206. You had about 275 when you were born. As you grow some smaller bones fuse together to form larger, stronger ones. More than half your bones are in your hands and feet. Your thigh bone, or femur, is the largest. The ossicles, inside your ears, are the smallest. Bones protect your organs. And the marrow in the center of bones produces the red and white blood cells you need to live.

"IS THAT ME?"

Why do camels have humps? How long can a camel go without water?

WILL YOU BRING ME A GLASS OF WATER, PLEASE?

Camels are built for long, dry journeys. Their humps are for fat storage. When food is short, they use up the fat for energy. Their stomach lining is specially built for water storage. How long camels can go without a drink depends on their travel speed and the weight of the load they're carrying. It's about 6 to 10 days if traveling is slow and easy.

Who kept the world's longest diary?

A very old person. Colonel Ernest Loftus, of Zimbabwe, began writing in his diary when he was 12 years old. He kept it up for 91 years until he died in 1987. He was 103.

Why do flowers have such bright colors?

To attract the birds and the bees so the flowers can be pollinated (fertilized) and produce seeds. Most flowers rely on insects and birds to carry their pollen. The visitors brush against the pollen and carry it on their bodies from one part of the flower to another, or from one flower to another.

HOW FAST IS THE

HOW LONG CAN A SNAKE GET?

If the snake could stand on its tail and you were at a window on the third story of a building, about 30 feet up, the snake could look you in the eye! This long, *long* snake could be an anaconda or a reticulated python, but fortunately, both stick to the ground.

WHO INVENTED SURFING?

People began surfing before anyone thought to record it. Hawaiians were catching waves when Captain Cook discovered the islands in 1778. They used big, heavy boards in those days. When smaller, lightweight boards were invented in the 1930s, surfing took off.

SPEED OF LIGHT?

Incredibly fast—faster than anyone can imagine. Light travels at a speed of about 186,000 miles per second. The circumference of the Earth (the distance around the world) is about 24,800 miles. That means light could travel around the world about seven and a half times in a single second!

DO YOU WANT TO RACE?

OKAY!

WHAT INSECT FLIES THE FASTEST?

The dragonfly. When a dragonfly comes by, duck! It can travel as fast as 30 miles per hour. But compared to many insects, this big bug beats its wings slowly—only about 25 to 40 beats per second. When a tiny mosquito takes off, it beats its wings (buzzzz!) about 600 beats per second, but only travels about one mile per hour.

DRAW ME!

Who was Walt Disney?

Mickey Mouse's "father." Disney (1901-1966) was a famous filmmaker. His first creation was Mickey Mouse. In 1928, Mickey starred in Disney's first sound cartoon, *Steamboat Willie*, and Disney was his voice.

Disney created the first full-length cartoon, *Snow White and the Seven Dwarfs*, in 1937. He built Disneyland theme park in California in 1955. Disneyworld, near Orlando, Florida, was opened in 1971.

HI, ROSE!

Why do plants have thorns?
Why do cacti have needles?

HI, CACTI!

It's a jungle out there, and plants have to defend themselves. Thorns and needles are the weapons of the plant world. Any animal that takes a bite out of a cactus is *not* coming back for a second helping.

WHAT'S AT THE CENTER OF THE EARTH?

THAT'S HOT!!

Hot stuff. Scientists believe the Earth has four layers. The *crust,* or solid rock, goes down about 20 miles (that's about five miles beneath the oceans). The next layer, the *mantle,* is about 1,800 miles deep. Then we come to the outer core, which is 1,400 miles of hot, liquid rock. And finally, to the core, 800 miles thick, a ball of hot, hot, 12,000 degrees Fahrenheit hot, solid rock.

WHAT ARE SEASHELLS MADE OF?

"Skeletons." Mollusks, like snails and clams, have their skeletons on the outside of their soft bodies instead of on the inside. They are shells —mostly made of limestone, a substance shellfish take from the water and convert into shell material. These skeletons grow as they grow. A mollusk is attached to its shell, so if a shell is empty, the animal is gone for good.

WHAT HAPPENS WHEN WATER BOILS?

It disappears. Actually, at 212°Fahrenheit (100°Celsius), water changes to steam, which is a gas. All liquids become gases when heated to a certain point. Heat loosens the bonds between a liquid's molecules, and they spread apart, becoming a light, thin gas. At 32°F (0°C), water's molecules slow down and bind together into solid ice.

IS THAT ONE OF US?

WHO WAS THE FIRST PERSON TO SET FOOT ON THE MOON?

Neil Armstrong, pilot of *Apollo 11*. On July 20, 1969, he and Buzz Aldrin rode the *Eagle*, a vehicle that detached from the main spacecraft, and landed on an area of the moon called the Sea of Tranquillity. As he put his foot on the moon's surface, he said, "That's one small step for [a] man, one giant leap for mankind."

WHAT IS THE WORLD'S TALLEST MOUNTAIN?

Mount Everest in the Himalayas on the border of Tibet and Nepal. It's 29,028 feet high. In 1953, Edmund Hillary and Tenzing Norgay were the first people ever to reach the top. In 1978, Reinhold Messner and Peter Habeler were the first to succeed without using bottled oxygen. The air gets very thin up there and breathing is difficult.

Why does a year have 365 days?

The number of days in the year is based on the sun. A solar day is the length of time it takes the Earth to rotate on its axis one time. A solar year is the number of solar days it takes for the Earth to revolve around the sun once. That number is exactly 365 days, 5 hours, 48 minutes, and 46 seconds. This explains leap years, which have 366 days. After four years, those extra five or so hours add up to a full day.

Who was Alexander the Great?

Alexander the Great got his name the hard way. He fought for it. Alexander was born in 356 B.C. and was only 20 years old when he became ruler of Macedonia, which is north of Greece. He set out to conquer the world and built an empire as big as the United States. It extended from Greece to Egypt and as far east east as India. And he did it all in 13 years! Alexander died when he was only 33.

WHAT MAKES LIGHTNING?

WHAT MAKES THUNDER?

Lightning is electricity on the loose. During a storm, strong air currents cause raindrops and pieces of hail to bang into each other, creating electricity. Enormous electric charges build up in clouds and on the ground. This ignites a giant spark between them—*lightning!* The lightning bolt heats up the air around it. Air particles expand and contract so quickly that they crash together and send out huge sound waves—*thunder!* The fastest lightning flashes are 87,000 miles per second!

Why did the dinosaurs die out?

Dinosaurs lived on the Earth for so long (about 160 million years!) and so successfully that scientists aren't sure why they died out. There are plenty of theories. A heat wave: changes in the Earth's climate may have made it too hot for plants and animals. A cold front: the dust from crashing meteorites could have blocked out the sun. Sunburn: volcanoes could have burnt through the Earth's protective ozone layer, letting through deadly ultraviolet radiation. Other theories say the extinctions were due to disease, sea-level changes, shifting continents, and mammals that ate dinosaur eggs. Which answer is right? We may never know for sure.

Why do dolphins seem smart?

They're brainy. A dolphin's brain, in relation to its body size, is as big as a human's. But a dolphin's brain is much simpler than the human brain. Dolphins are naturally curious and playful. They learn quickly and even understand some language. Because this behavior seems "human," we think they're smart. And, in their way, they are.

WHAT'S THE SMELLIEST THING IN THE WORLD?

There are thousands of smells in the world and millions of opinions on what is the worst. The cause of a nasty smell is its chemical combination. For example, rotten eggs could be one of the smelliest things in the world. The odor is from *sulfur dioxide*. And if you ever come across the chemical *ethyl mercaptan* you won't forget it. It is said to smell like a combination of rotting cabbage, garlic, onions, burned toast, and sewer gas.

HOW DO WAVES FORM IN THE OCEAN?

Waves start with wind, not water. Picture the wind moving across the surface of the ocean, lifting the water. When the wind blows harder, the waves get bigger. When the winds are calm, waves are usually no more than a few feet high. But in a storm, they may be whipped up to 60 feet tall. One of the highest waves recorded in the Pacific Ocean was 112 feet high—a wall of water taller than a 10-story building!

WHO WAS HOUDINI?

The greatest escape artist of all time. Harry Houdini (1874-1926) was a magician who created contraptions of ropes, handcuffs, tires, and chains from which only he could escape. He was nailed inside boxes. He was trapped in water-filled tanks. He was wrapped up in a straight-jacket and dropped in the ocean. But he always got free.

HOW DOES A ROCKET SOUND IN SPACE?

Like one hand clapping—there's no sound at all. Sound is created by "sound waves," a movement of the molecules that make up air. In space there is no air. Therefore, there are no waves and no sound.

101

How does a firefighter put out a fire?

As quickly as possible, and it depends on the fire. Any fire must have fuel, heat, and oxygen. A wood, paper, or fabric fire is put out with powerful streams of water, which absorbs the heat. But water can't put out an electrical fire because it conducts electricity. And water doesn't mix with oil, grease, or gas, so it's not useful for those fires. Grease and electrical fires are snuffed out with carbon dioxide, which cuts off the fire's oxygen. Gas fires are fought with water fog, a spray of fine water particles, and foam. These form a blanket over the fire and smother it.

What causes chicken pox?

You usually catch it from a friend, because it's *contagious*. The scientific name is "varicella," and the cause is a virus. Once you've got it, there's not much to do but wait until it's over—and try not to scratch. Chicken pox is itchy. The pox are small skin eruptions that make your skin look a little like a chicken's.

CAN I GET PEOPLE POX?

WHO WERE THE GLADIATORS?

I'D RATHER HAVE PIZZA!!

The Roman Empire was a great civilization with a cruel form of entertainment—the fighting of gladiators. These men were prisoners of war, slaves, or criminals. They were forced to fight each other in a great stadium while the Romans cheered. Most of the time, the gladiators battled until one gruesomely killed the other. These fights were usually part of festivals that sometimes went on for months. All this "fun" lasted from 264 B.C. to A.D. 404.

WHAT MAKES A DIAMOND SPARKLE?

You can't have sparkle without light, and diamonds make the most of it. A diamond is a pure carbon crystal formed beneath the earth under severe heat and pressure. But it doesn't sparkle in its natural form. Diamond cutters cut *facets*—small surfaces—into the stone that catch the light. A cut diamond has the ability to bend the light and reflect it more than any other substance, and that makes it sparkle.

Have aliens ever visited Earth?

Scientists have no evidence that extraterrestrial beings have ever been on our planet. But that doesn't stop some people from believing that aliens have dropped by now and then. There have been many claims of UFO sightings around the world, and a few folks even claim to have been abducted by aliens!

Dear Mom,
Having a wonderful time
on earth—wish
you were here!
Love,
GORZAT II

MOM,
MARS 10013

The idea is so fascinating to real believers that they don't need scientific proof to think it's true.

103

THIS IS NOT MY LUCKY DAY!!

What are spittlebugs?

Not too many bugs are a pretty sight, but spittlebugs are stuck with an ugly name. "Spittle" is a word for the bubbly saliva mess we all think of as "spit." Spittlebugs are small jumping insects, less than half an inch long, that look like tiny frogs. In their *nymph*, or infant stage, they live in a frothy, spittlelike mass, which they create themselves. So "spittlebug," after all, is a name they deserve.

WHY DO WE GET GOOSEBUMPS?

When we get cold, the hairs on our body stand up straight. When this happens, our skin pushes up into little bumps. Our body may be trying to keep us warm, but the hairs we have just don't do the trick! If we had fur or feathers that stood on end, the air between them would hold in the heat and keep the cold out. So, unfortunately, we remain cold and simply look like geese whose feathers have just been plucked.

WHO INVENTED ICE CREAM?

It remains a mystery. Most historians agree that Italy's Catherine de Medici, with help from chef Bernardo Buontalenti, introduced "cream ice" to France in 1533. The cold, creamy confection wasn't known as "ice cream" until it reached America in the 1700s, where it became wildly popular. First president George Washington spent a great deal of money on the expensive dessert. He even liked to make it at home with a "Cream Machine for Making Ice." The price dropped a century later when Jacob Fussell, a Baltimore dairyman, invented the first ice-cream factory.

WHY IS

CONSIDERED AN UNLUCKY NUMBER?

Poor number 13. People have been uneasy about it since primitive man counted his ten fingers and two feet and came up with 12. After that came the unknown—13. And anything unknown is scary. As with all superstitions, there is no reasonable answer. But that doesn't mean people don't take it seriously. Many hotels and office buildings don't have a 13th floor!

What happens to bears when they hibernate?

Not much. When most animals hibernate, their body temperature drops and their breathing slows down. Not bears. They just sleep away most of the winter in a normal, but very drowsy, state. Cubs are born in the winter, and the mothers practically sleep through the whole ordeal! Everyone may get up and walk around for awhile, but then it's back to the den to sleep until spring.

DO NOT DISTURB

Z-Z-Z-Z-

Has anyone ever found pirate's treasure?

Yes! More than 100,000 objects were recovered from the *Whydah*, a ship captured in 1717 by the pirate Samuel Bellamy off the coast of the Bahamas. The shipwrecked vessel was *salvaged*, or brought up from the sea, in 1984. Among the treasures was a collection of gold jewelry, created by the Akan people of Africa.

WHAT IS AIR MADE OF?

It feels like nothing, but air is definitely something. It's invisible, but it's not weightless. Air is made up of gases, mostly nitrogen and some oxygen with a small amount of argon. There's also a bit of water vapor. A hundred miles of air rises above your head—or sits on your shoulders.

DOES A CAT REALLY HAVE NINE LIVES?

It just seems that way. Cats are fast and flexible—and they have an excellent sense of balance. They bound out of the way of danger. They fall from scary heights and land on their feet. They squeeze out of tight spots. Cats escape harm so often that people say they have "nine lives."

WHY DO FLIES HAVE SUCH BIG EYES?

"The better to see you with, my dear." Most insects have large eyes made up of many lenses. These are called *compound eyes*. (Some dragonflies have 300,000 lenses in each eye!) In fact, flies don't see too clearly because each lens is fixed and can't be adjusted for distance. But flies with eyes that cover most of their heads have 360-degree vision. They can see anything coming at them from any-where—which is why it's so hard to catch a fly.

What happens to the garbage I throw away?

All 1,300 pounds? That's about how much garbage each one of us throws away every year. Some solid waste goes into landfills. These are low areas where towns build mountains of garbage. The piles are packed down and covered with dirt. Very slowly, over years, tiny living organisms called microbes break down the garbage and it decays. Some solid waste is burned in huge furnaces called incinerators. Other garbage can be *recycled*. Metal objects, such as cans, are crushed, shredded, cleaned, and melted. Then the metal is recycled, or used again. Newspapers, bottles, and plastics are also recycled.

Are all sharks dangerous?

No—but never test a shark to find out. Fewer than a hundred people worldwide are attacked by sharks each year. Twenty kinds of sharks have been known to attack people, and a few others are considered dangerous. Whale sharks are the most friendly. They can weigh more than 30,000 pounds, but they're so gentle, sometimes divers hold on to their fins and take a ride.

HOW CAN APES LEARN SIGN LANGUAGE?

I GET TO CELEBRATE BOTH FATHER'S AND MOTHER'S DAY!

DO MALE ANIMALS EVER GIVE BIRTH?

No, but the sea horse does a pretty good imitation. Sea horses are fish with scaly bodies and curved tails. And they're tiny—the smallest are only 2 inches and the largest are nearly a foot long. The male doesn't give birth, but he sure looks pregnant. He has a pouch just above his tail where the female places her eggs. Then she takes off and he carries the eggs around in his bulging belly for 40 to 50 days. He even takes care of the babies after they hatch.

WHAT'S THE DIFFERENCE BETWEEN A MOTH AND A BUTTERFLY?

Night flight... Moths fly mostly at dark and butterflies during the day. *Antennae...* Butterflies have long, knob-tipped antennae and moths have feathery ones. *Body shape...* Butterflies are slim and moths are chunky. But if you pick up either by the wings, you may get a fine dust on your fingers. These are the scales that prove that, despite their differences, both belong to the same group of "scaly-winged" creatures, the Lepidoptera.

Apes learn sign language based on the hand signals that deaf people use. The apes watch their trainer's hands, imitate the movements, and get a reward when they get it right. Apes can even put two signs together to make a phrase like "Want food." And, using sign language, they can "talk" to each other. A famous gorilla named Koko was the first member of her species to communicate using sign language. Since 1972 she has learned more than 1,000 signs. That's an ape with a lot to say!

What happens when a space shuttle returns to Earth's atmosphere?

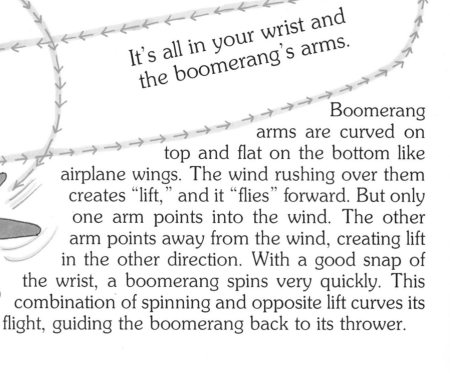

It's a hot moment. When the shuttle enters Earth's atmosphere, gravity takes hold and the surrounding air causes enormous friction. Friction causes heat. In this case, the fiery temperature is more than we can imagine—3,000°F. The shuttle is protected by special tiles on its underside. They are so good at shedding heat that they can be burning hot on one side and cool enough to touch on the other.

WHY DOES A BOOMERANG COME BACK?

I JUST CAN'T SEEM TO THROW IT AWAY!!!

It's all in your wrist and the boomerang's arms.

Boomerang arms are curved on top and flat on the bottom like airplane wings. The wind rushing over them creates "lift," and it "flies" forward. But only one arm points into the wind. The other arm points away from the wind, creating lift in the other direction. With a good snap of the wrist, a boomerang spins very quickly. This combination of spinning and opposite lift curves its flight, guiding the boomerang back to its thrower.

What happens when the sun sets?

GOOD NIGHT!

Nothing happens to the sun. It stays in the same place while the Earth turns on its *axis* (an imaginary line from the North Pole to the South Pole). When the Earth makes one complete turn, a day has passed. Only half the planet can be facing the sun at one time. As that side turns away from the sun, we say the sun is setting. Then we are in darkness until "tomorrow," when our place on Earth turns back to the sun again.

WHAT IS A SLOTH?

A slow-moving, furry mammal that lives in the tropical forests of Central and South America. It lives in the trees—eating, sleeping, and maneuvering upside down, clinging with sharp claws. Sloths rarely move faster than six feet a minute. If they do come down from a tree, they only hurry—well, sort of—to another tree.

Who created the first zoo?

First, think of what a zoo is for—a chance to enjoy watching animals and to study their habits. A Chinese emperor created such a place 3,000 years ago. His small collection of animals could be called the first zoo. Today, the best zoos want their animals to feel at home, so they create environments similar to an animal's natural surroundings. A zoo also works to save species that are in danger of extinction.

111

WHAT ARE THE SEVEN WONDERS

Amazing human-made structures, most of which no longer exist.

The Great Pyramids at Giza, Egypt, are the only surviving ancient wonder. Tombs of pharaohs, they were built around 2600 B.C. by thousands of laborers. The Great Pyramid of Khufu is the largest, covering about 13 acres and standing 482 feet high.

The Hanging Gardens of Babylon were built around 600 B.C. for the queen of Babylon. The ancient city of Babylon was located close to where Baghdad, Iraq, is today. Early writings tell us that the gardens were laid out on a 300-square-foot brick terrace about 75 feet above the ground. Laborers worked around the clock to lift water from the Euphrates River to water the flowers.

WHO MOWS THE LAWN?

The Temple of Artemis at Ephesus was built around 550 B.C. in the Greek city of Ephesus to honor the goddess Artemis. All marble, it was one of the most complicated temples ever built in ancient times. It had 127 columns, each 60 feet high.

OF THE ANCIENT WORLD?

The **Colossus of Rhodes** was a huge bronze statue in the city of Rhodes in ancient Greece. It was built to honor Helios, the sun god. It took 12 years to complete and was probably 120 feet tall, about the same size as the Statue of Liberty. In 224 B.C., the statue was destroyed by an earthquake.

The Statue of Zeus was built around 435 B.C. in Olympia, Greece. Zeus was the king of the gods in ancient Greece—and this statue fit his role. It was said to be 40 feet high. Zeus was carved in ivory sitting on his throne in royal robes made of gold.

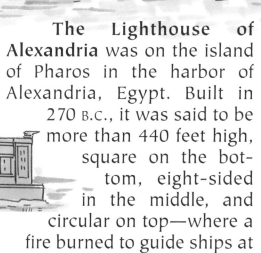

The **Lighthouse of Alexandria** was on the island of Pharos in the harbor of Alexandria, Egypt. Built in 270 B.C., it was said to be more than 440 feet high, square on the bottom, eight-sided in the middle, and circular on top—where a fire burned to guide ships at night.

The Mausoleum at Halicarnassus was built around 353 B.C. in what is now Turkey. The marble tomb was constructed for Mausolus, an official of the Persian Empire. The tomb became so famous that large tombs are now called *mausoleums*.

How **big** *is a baby whale?*

Bigger than any other baby on Earth. The largest whale is the blue whale and its baby is the biggest. At birth, these babies can be 20 to 26 feet long and weigh more than 6,000 pounds. Just one year later they can grow to 28 tons!

HOW DOES A REMOTE CONTROL WORK?

Invisibly—with infrared light rays and electricity. If you want to change the channel on your TV, you press a button on the remote control unit and send a beam of infrared rays to the receiver unit in the TV. The beam contains a signal made up of electrical pulses. The receiver detects the signal. Then it "decodes" the signal and changes the channel.

WHO INVENTED CHEWING GUM?

The stuff of "chewing" gum is chicle (CHEE-clay), the gum of the sapodilla tree. The Aztec Indians of Mexico chewed it to clean their teeth. In 1872, Thomas Adams mixed sugar and flavor with chicle and created a rubbery candy. Actually, he was looking for a substitute for rubber when he popped a piece of chicle into his mouth. He chewed on his idea for a while and out popped gum!

ZAP!

HOW DOES HAIL FORM?

A hailstone forms when a drop of moisture from a cloud gets tossed in the wind. An "updraft" catches the drop and swings it upward where the temperature is below freezing. The drop freezes, then falls into the cloud again. It's blown back up. Another layer of ice is added. This ping-pong effect can go on and on until an ice pellet is heavy enough to plunge to the ground. Huge hailstones can smash roofs, break windows, and even harm people. One hailstone that fell to Earth weighed two and a half pounds!

OUCH!

Does it hurt a woodpecker to hammer on a tree?

No. Woodpeckers are hard-headed. They have thick skulls that can take the banging, and strong neck muscles that absorb the shock. Woodpeckers drill holes to get at the insects inside trees.

OH, NO! HAIL!!

What makes a flower smell good?

All plants and animals have characteristics or behaviors that help them reproduce. In order to grow seeds, flowers must transfer pollen from their male parts to their female parts. Insects often carry the pollen. And flowers attract the insects with their smells. The perfume comes from tiny particles called scent strips on the petals and other parts of the flower.

When did women first compete in sports?

For most of history, the two words "women" and "sports" didn't go together. But the world is constantly changing. Women first competed in the Olympic Games in golf and tennis in 1900. They wore long skirts, which certainly didn't help their games. As time went on, women began competing in almost all the sports that men have been playing for centuries.

HOW DOES A TADPOLE TURN INTO A FROG?

Metamorphosis (met-ah-MORE-foh-sis). That's the big word for change in an animal's body. Frogs begin life as tadpoles—tiny, tailed, fishlike creatures that breathe with gills in the water. As tadpoles grow, rear legs appear, then front legs. Then the tail disappears and the creature *looks* like a frog. But it is not until lungs replace the gills that the tadpole *becomes* a frog—an animal that breathes air on land. Some frogs metamorphose in days or weeks. The big, noisy bullfrog takes nearly a year.

WHAT IS VIRTUAL REALITY?

Reality is reading this book. Or sitting in a chair. Or anything that happens to you. Virtual Reality (VR, for short) is not real life, but it can be close. People create VR with computers. They feed the computer information. The computer turns the facts into visual images that behave and move as if they were real. To "feel" the virtual world, you might wear a headset or goggles, a computerized vest, or a pair of gloves. Your chair might be attached to the computer. If you were on a roller coaster in virtual reality, you would feel the sensations of the ride. You would be plunged into a new "unreal" reality.

DO ANY REAL HAUNTED HOUSES EXIST?

It's spooky, but many people think they do. The Winchester House in California is a big house actually built for ghosts. Sarah Winchester, heiress to the Winchester rifle fortune, was told by a psychic that a curse had been placed on her by the ghosts of people killed by the rifles. To get rid of the curse, the psychic told Sarah to build a house for the spirits. At the end of 38 years the house had 160 rooms and 950 doors! In her will, Sarah insisted that ghosts always be welcomed there. Want to visit?

WE'LL TAKE IT!

FOR RENT

WHAT MAKES SPECIAL EFFECTS ON TV AND IN THE MOVIES SO REAL?

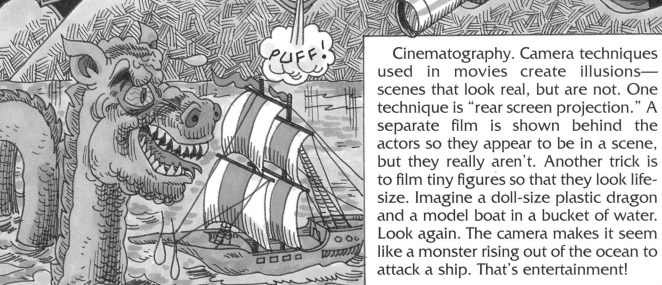

PUFF!

Cinematography. Camera techniques used in movies create illusions—scenes that look real, but are not. One technique is "rear screen projection." A separate film is shown behind the actors so they appear to be in a scene, but they really aren't. Another trick is to film tiny figures so that they look life-size. Imagine a doll-size plastic dragon and a model boat in a bucket of water. Look again. The camera makes it seem like a monster rising out of the ocean to attack a ship. That's entertainment!

What are feathers made of?

Keratin, a protein, the same substance that you have in your hair and nails. Feathers on a bird are called plumage, and they can be beautiful colors—red, yellow, brown, even blue and violet. But they're not just for decoration. Feathers are for flying.

I'M REALLY BEAUTIFUL!

I'M EVERMORE BEAUTIFUL!

NO, I'M BEAUTIFUL!

I'M THE MOST BEAUTIFUL!

I'M BEAUTIFUL!

HOW DO I REMEMBER THINGS?

Think of your brain as a gigantic computer, but much more complicated. Nerve cells take in information and pass it back and forth. Suppose you eat a peach for the first time. Nerves in your eyes, nose, and mouth pass along news to your brain about how a peach looks, smells, and tastes. Your brain records the word "peach" and the experience of eating it. The next time you think of a peach your brain will call up the stored information.

Who invented chess?

The earliest recorded chess games were played in Persia about 1,500 years ago. The term "checkmate" comes from the Persian phrase *shah mat,* which means "the king cannot escape." The Arabs learned chess when they conquered Persia in the 7th century A.D., and then brought the game to Spain, from where it spread throughout Europe. International tournaments began in 1851.

WHERE IS THE RING OF FIRE?

Where the volcanoes are. The Ring of Fire describes the area where more than 75 percent of the world's 850 active volcanoes are. The boundaries are where the earth's crust under the Pacific Ocean meets the continents. The "ring" goes from Alaska in North America to Chile in South America on one side and from Siberia to New Zealand on the other. The most volcanoes are in Indonesia—a very hot spot.

VOLCANO!

HOW DOES A RADIO WORK?

Radio waves do the work. They are electromagnetic waves in the air that vibrate at different rates, or frequencies. Radio signals pass along these waves at incredible speeds, faster than the speed of light, nearly 190,000 miles per second. At the radio station, words or music are turned into electrical signals and sent from an antenna, along a radio wave frequency, to your radio. When you turn on that station's number, you are tuning into that frequency and receiving its signal.

VOLCANO!

119

HOW MANY GALAXIES ARE IN THE UNIVERSE?

8 BILLION
AND 2...
8 BILLION
AND 3...
8 BILLION
AND 4...

Billions—more than we can see with even the most powerful telescopes. Each galaxy is a huge collection of gas, dust, and, probably, billions of stars, all held together by gravity. The sun and its planets, including Earth, are part of a galaxy called the Milky Way. Look for a hazy band of bright stars across the night sky and you may see part of it.

HOW IS A HOLOGRAM MADE?

With lasers, light, and mirrors that play tricks with our eyes. A hologram is really a flat image, but it looks three-dimensional. Special photographic film is used to develop the picture. First, an object is lit by a laser beam. One part of the beam reflects off the object onto the photographic plate. Another part of the beam reflects off mirrors onto the plate. When the plate is developed, it records the two images. Then, when we look at the picture in certain lights, it appears as if the image is three-dimensional and has depth.

PHOTOGRAPHIC PLATE

PHOTOGRAPHIC PLATE

BURP!

WHY DO WE BURP?

EXCUSE ME!

It's the body's way of getting rid of the air we "eat." When you take a big gulp of food, you're treating your stomach to air along with it. When you drink a fizzy soda, those air-filled bubbles bounce around in your belly. Sometimes the entrance valve to the stomach opens and the air rushes up. It vibrates in the throat and makes the noise we call—excuse me—a burp.

Who was the first African-American to play baseball in the major leagues?

Jackie Robinson, a real sports hero. When he began playing for the Brooklyn Dodgers in 1947, he was the only African-American in baseball. Unfortunately, there were still a lot of people who thought he didn't belong. But he stood up for what was right. He played for 10 years and helped his team win six National League pennants. In 1962, Jackie Robinson became the first African-American to enter the National Baseball Hall of Fame.

WHAT IS DÉJÀ VU?

ⱾUV ÁƐ̀ЀD ƧI TAHW

Have you ever been someplace for the first time but had the feeling you'd been there before? Have you ever met a stranger and felt like you'd met him or her before? This odd feeling is called déjà vu. The word comes from the French *déjà*, which means "already," plus *vu*, which means "seen."

WHAT DO DIFFERENT COLORS SYMBOLIZE?

It depends where you are. Colors often have different meanings in different countries. For example, in the United States, red stands for danger—stop signs are red. And it symbolizes love—hearts are red. But it can also mean anger, as in "I saw red!" In China, however, red is the color of happiness. In the U.S., brides wear white to their weddings. In China, mourners wear white to funerals.

WHO MADE THE FIRST MAP?

YOU ARE HERE

Someone who wasn't going too far. The first known map was a clay tablet that shows a portion of the Euphrates River in Mesopotamia, which is now Iraq. That was around 2300 B.C. The most famous ancient maps were made by Claudius Ptolemy, an Egyptian scholar. Around A.D. 150 he drew a map of the world as it was known at that time. He included regional maps of Europe, Africa, and Asia. The whole Western Hemisphere was yet to be discovered. In other words, we weren't on the map.

What was Mark Twain's real name?

Samuel Clemens. One of America's greatest writers, he lived from 1835 to 1910, and his books are just as much fun today as they were a century ago. Two of his stories, *The Adventures of Tom Sawyer* and *The Adventures of Huckleberry Finn*, are among the best-known novels in American fiction.

WHEN WAS THE FIRST BOOK PRINTED?

The first book was "printed" in China in A.D. 868 with wooden blocks dipped in ink. Other wooden block systems were invented, but they were too slow and difficult to use to create many books. In 15th-century Germany, Johannes Gutenberg invented a way to print with metal blocks that moved around and could be used again and again. In 1455, with this first printing press, he produced copies of the Gutenberg Bible. For the first time, books were available to many people.

HOW DO PICTURES AND SOUND GET ONTO MY TV SCREEN?

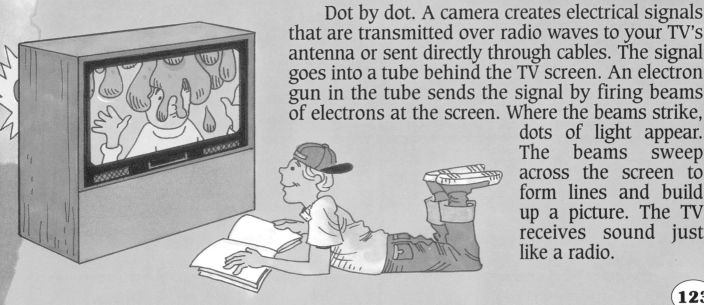

Dot by dot. A camera creates electrical signals that are transmitted over radio waves to your TV's antenna or sent directly through cables. The signal goes into a tube behind the TV screen. An electron gun in the tube sends the signal by firing beams of electrons at the screen. Where the beams strike, dots of light appear. The beams sweep across the screen to form lines and build up a picture. The TV receives sound just like a radio.

What is the largest fish?

OOPS!!

THAT'S A WHALE OF A SHARK!

COMING THROUGH!

What happens to the water I drink?

GULP!

It goes to work. About half your blood is made up of water, which moves blood cells through your veins and arteries. Water also plays a big role in your organs. For example, water in your liver helps process digested foods. Water in your kidneys helps filter waste out of your blood. And water in your urine carries the waste out of your body. A grown man has 10 quarts of water circulating in his body every day.

WHO INVENTED CHEESE?

Cheese is an ancient food. Experts believe it was first eaten in the Middle East. It seems likely that someone who raised cows, goats, or sheep first made cheese by accident. When milk sours it separates into curds (soft clumps), and whey (liquid). The curds can be aged into cheese. The Sumerians, a people that thrived 6,000 years ago in the area that is now Iraq, were probably the first cheese lovers.

The whale shark—a gentle giant you don't have to be afraid of (it only eats tiny sea creatures). One of the largest whale sharks ever captured was more than 40 feet long and weighed about 33,000 pounds. They may be big, but whale sharks are rarely seen.

WHY DO THE DAYS GET LONGER AND SHORTER DURING THE YEAR?

We're spinning. Earth spins, or rotates, tilted on its *axis*, an imaginary line from the North Pole to the South Pole. Earth also makes a complete circle around the sun each year. These two motions constantly put us in a different position, relative to the sun. During part of the year, the North Pole tilts toward the sun, causing longer days in the Northern Hemisphere. When the South Pole tilts toward the sun, the Southern Hemisphere has longer days. But it happens gradually as Earth's position shifts. So each day the amount of light reaching your part of the world changes just slightly.

Why did castles have moats?

It was one more way to keep enemies out! In the Middle Ages, landowners in Europe fought over their territory. These "land lords" built their castles as forts, with high stone walls for protection. But to keep enemies from climbing the walls, the castle was surrounded by a moat, a deep ditch usually filled with water. A moat was crossed by a drawbridge that could be raised from within the castle.

125

What is an ENDANGERED animal?

If an animal species is close to extinction and there are so few left in the world, it is said to be endangered. An animal becomes endangered for many reasons. Pollution may ruin its territory. Cutting down forests may destroy its habitat. Hunting may wipe out its population. Chemicals may poison its food source. But people can make a big difference. In 1987, there were only 27 California Condors left. Conservationists captured and bred the rare birds in an attempt to recover their population. Through conservation efforts, many endangered animals have been rescued, including the bald eagle, the bison, and the American alligator.

Why does it hurt to pull your hair but not to cut it?

The hair on your head is dead. Each hair starts growing below the skin in a follicle that contains a root. New cells in the root divide and force older cells upward. That's when the older hair cells die and harden into the hair you see on your head. The hair below the skin is alive and surrounded by nerves. Pull it and you'll feel it!

SNIP! SNIP! SNIP!

What is the coldest place on Earth?

About 800 miles from the South Pole in Antarctica. That's where the lowest temperature has been recorded. In July 1983, on a day when you might have been swimming, the temperature in Vostok was -129°F. Don't even think about the windchill factor!

MOM DID TELL ME TO BUNDLE UP!

What causes an avalanche?

The wind can trigger an avalanche, but so can melting snow, or a sudden loud sound like a rifle shot. The rest is all downhill—tons of snow, ice, mud, or rock crashing down a mountainside. The wind created by an avalanche can be enormous. In 1970, an avalanche in Peru swept through towns and villages, killing at least 18,000 people on its way.

FEET, DO YOUR THING!!

Which famous composer of music was deaf?

Ludwig van Beethoven (1770-1827)—one of the greatest composers who ever lived. Even as a young German boy his talents were recognized by major artists. He began to lose his hearing at age 30, and his world was silent by age 47. But he kept right on composing, and left the world the gift of his music.

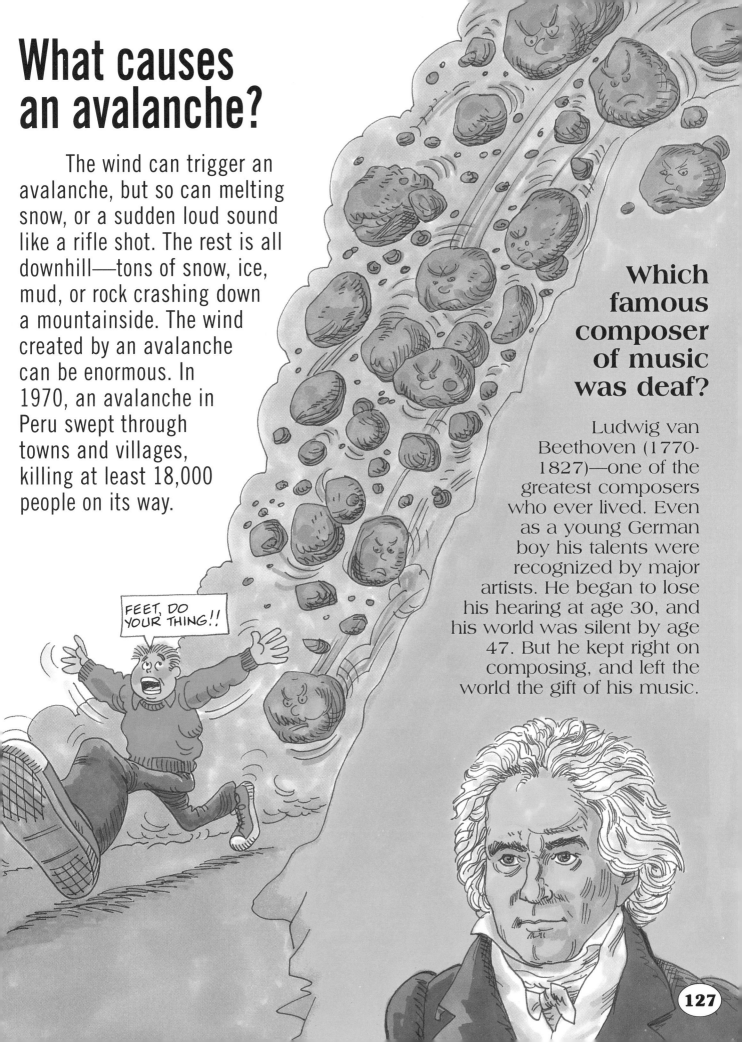

WHAT DOES IT MEAN TO BE DOUBLE-JOINTED?

Nothing. Every elbow, knee, ankle, and shoulder is a spot where two bones meet and a joint connects them. Fingers and toes have many joints. Some people can bend these joints in pretty amazing ways. But they've got the same amount of joints as the rest of us. They're just more flexible.

HOW DOES MY HEART WORK?

Automatically—and it never gets tired. Your heart is a powerful muscle that pumps blood around your body. It's made up of two types of muscle, *striated* (voluntary) and *smooth* (involuntary). Smooth muscle allows the heart to beat regularly. Blood travels through veins and arteries to and from your heart. Arteries carry oxygen-rich blood to every part of your body. Veins carry blood back to your heart to pick up more oxygen. As your heart does its job, the cycle occurs over and over again.

ARTERIES TO HEAD, ARMS, AND NECK

AORTA

PULMONARY ARTERY

SUPERIOR VENA CAVA

VALVE

LEFT ATRIUM

LEFT VENTRICLE

RIGHT PULMONARY VEINS

RIGHT ATRIUM

INFERIOR VENA CAVA

RIGHT VENTRICLE

SEPTUM

IT DOESN'T LOOK LIKE A HEART!

Why do we blink?

To keep our eyes clean. Tear glands under our upper eyelids make tears all the time. When we blink, thousands of times a day, we spread the tears to wash away dust and dirt. Our eyelashes also keep things from entering our eyes. But we can also blink on purpose, as if to say "Just kidding!" That's called winking!

WHY DO WE LAUGH ?

Because it feels good and helps us relax. What we laugh at is another story. You could giggle yourself silly over something that your friend thinks is stupid or boring or even insulting. But once you get started, it's hard to stop. Laughter is one of the automatic responses your body takes care of on its own. Your stomach tenses up. Your face scrunches up. Tears squeeze out of your tear glands. And when it's over, you feel good!

How do we grow?

Slowly. Our pituitary gland, located at the bottom of the brain, sets the pace. One of the hormones, or chemicals, it releases stimulates growth, causing our cells to divide and multiply. The more cells there are, the more of us there is! Scientists aren't sure why we stop growing, but fortunately there seems to be a limit.

129

What's the difference between a ROCK and a MINERAL?

A rock is solid material made up of minerals. A mineral forms from chemical combinations in the earth. Salt is one type of mineral. Minerals may be hard or soft, shiny or dull. They may be colorful, and they may conduct heat or electricity. Minerals in different combinations form different types of rocks. Marble, a very hard rock, and chalk, a soft powdery substance, both contain the same mineral—calcium carbonate.

What causes freckles?

Melanin, a naturally occurring brown substance, or *pigment*, found in everybody's skin. The amount of melanin we have determines our skin color. But sometimes our pigment cells produce melanin in clusters. We call these freckles.

Who invented the teddy bear?

I WAS NAMED AFTER HIM!

In 1902, President Teddy Roosevelt went hunting and refused to shoot a bear cub. A cartoonist drew a picture for a newspaper of the great president sparing the life of the little bear. Morris Michtom, a Brooklyn toy maker, thought the cartoon would help him sell stuffed bears. He was right. He put the bear in his window with the picture and called it "Teddy's Bear." Toys in America haven't been the same since. Presidents have come and gone, a century has passed, and the teddy bear is still going strong.

WHERE DO PIÑATAS COME FROM?

South of the border, from Central and South America. Piñatas filled with candy or toys are now found at children's parties all over the world. Often made of papier-mâché in the shape of an animal, piñatas are colorfully decorated and hung from a rope. The idea is to whack the piñata open with a stick or a bat. Sometimes the children are blindfolded, so the treats that spill out are really a surprise.

Do animals dream? Do babies?

Babies do, and they spend much more time dreaming than adults. One theory is that we dream to sort out new experiences, knitting them in with the rest of our lives. Babies have a new experience about every minute.

Animals, however, are a different matter. The brains of animals such as reptiles and fish are constructed much differently from ours, making them very difficult to study. But there have been experiments with other mammals, such as monkeys and cats, which seem to show that they dream. Just imagine if they could tell us what they dream about!

Because it's big—864,000 miles across—and it's HOT! The sun's core is hotter than you can imagine—about 30,000,000°F. *Thermonuclear* explosions, occurring at the sun's core, create heat and pressure that change hydrogen gas into helium. That process, called *fusion*, creates huge amounts of energy that burst to the surface, appearing as heat and light. This heat and light "shine" all the way to Earth, over 92 million miles away. It takes sunlight about eight minutes to get here.

AH! THAT FEELS GOOD!

I CAN'T EVEN FLY A KITE!

What would it be like to live on the MOON?

You'd be trapped in a space suit because there's no oxygen to breathe. The temperature on the moon ranges from scorching hot, a sizzling 216°F, to the ultimate frozen zone, -279°F! And one cycle from day to night is 27 Earth days.

How does a seed grow into a plant?

Germination—that's a big word for the sprouting of a seed. Seeds need the right temperature, moisture, and oxygen to germinate. First, water softens the seed coat, and the growing parts break out of the seed. A root grows downward. Then the stem bends upward and breaks through the soil. Small roots branch off the main root. Then the leaves develop and the plant is on its own.

Who was King Midas?

In Greek mythology, the god Dionysus gave Midas the ability to turn everything he touched into gold. But there was one problem—even his food turned to gold. Luckily, Dionysus took back his blessing. But the memory of Midas lives on in this saying about successful people: "They have the Midas touch."

WHAT HAPPENED DURING THE ICE AGES?

Ice covered large parts of the Earth. Scientists believe that ice ages occur every 150 million years or so due to changes in the global climate. During the last Ice Age, which ended about 10,000 years ago, parts of North America and Europe were covered with ice up to 9,800 feet thick! Glaciers, huge masses of moving ice, crushed forests, created mountains, and carved out valleys. As the global climate warmed, glaciers began to melt and receded toward the North and South Poles. Glaciers still exist in cold parts of the world, such as Greenland, Canada, and Antarctica.

Who was Joan of Arc?

A French farm girl who became a saint by fighting for her country. Jeanne d'Arc (1412-1431) lived at a time when France was at war with England and losing badly. Jeanne had visions that convinced her she could liberate France. She persuaded the king to allow her to lead men into battle—imagine a 17-year-old girl in armor giving orders to generals! She recaptured the city of Orléans and became a great hero. In the end, she was captured by her enemies and burned at the stake as a witch. In 1920, the Roman Catholic Church declared her a saint.

What's the difference between KARATE and TAE KWON DO?

Both are martial arts, Asian forms of unarmed combat. Karate developed in Okinawa, Japan, in the 17th century. Tae Kwon Do began in Korea around 50 B.C. Karate means "empty hand" and focuses on using the hands and arms. Tae Kwon Do means "the art of kicking and punching" and focuses more on leg power. Aside from self-defense and physical fitness, all martial arts set out to teach a way of life. Emphasis is on concentration, confidence, and harmony with nature. Fighting is the last option for solving a conflict in real life.

Where is the world's longest roller

IS EARTH THE ONLY PLANET THAT HAS A MOON?

Heavens, no! In our solar system nine planets circle the sun. Moons circle most of the planets—and that's many moons. Saturn has at least 22, and Jupiter at least 16. Uranus is right up there with at least 15 moons, and Neptune follows with 8 or more. Pluto has only one, but it's half the size of the planet. Only Mercury and Venus are out there alone.

I'M NOT THE ONLY ONE!

HOW DID THE LOST CONTINENT OF ATLANTIS GET LOST?

MY LITTLE JOKE!

It may have never existed. The Greek philosopher Plato (427-347 B.C.) wrote a story about a glorious island in the Atlantic Ocean that sank into the sea because of earthquakes and floods. Although Plato never claimed his tale was true, some people came to believe that Atlantis really existed.

THIS IS EASY!

NO PROBLEM.

EASY AS PIE!

NO BIG DEAL.

OH-OH!

Y!//////IKES!

Z

MAKE MY DAY!

In a place where stomachs drop and fear rises—Lightwater Valley Theme Park in England. The roller coaster is called The Ultimate. And at 1.42 miles, it certainly is.

coaster?

How does a gasoline engine work?

A gasoline engine creates the force of energy that gets a vehicle going. *Combustion* is the key—a quick explosion that creates heat. This heat creates energy. In a car engine, a mixture of air and gasoline is lit by a spark in a *cylinder* containing a *piston*. (Think of a can with a disk-shaped plunger that fits exactly inside.) The heat from this little explosion makes the air expand and forces down the piston. The piston turns the *crankshaft*, a rod that is linked to the wheels. The wheels turn and off you go!

How can penguins tell each other apart?

It's all beak speak. When thousands of look-alike penguins gather in the same place each year for mating, the males attract females by *calling*. Couples "sing" together to learn each other's unique voice. Next year, when they return, many penguins find their long-lost mates from the year before. Scientists believe they can recognize each other's voice.

Who invented BASKETBALL?

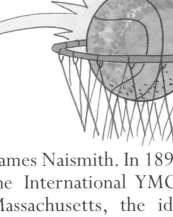

I DID!

A Canadian, Dr. James Naismith. In 1891, as an instructor at the International YMCA Training School in Massachusetts, the idea struck him. It was December and too cold to play outdoor sports. The game he created had nine players to a team, and the "hoops" were wooden peach baskets. Four years later basketball was played everywhere in the country. Now it's played practically everywhere in the world.

WHY DO I YAWN WHEN I GET SLEEPY?

To keep yourself up! A yawn is a slow, deep breath that brings more oxygen to the brain. It's a little like splashing cold water on your face. The oxygen gives your brain cells a little wake-up call.

WHAT'S THE HOTTEST SPICE IN THE WORLD?

It's a type of chile—the Red "Savina" habanero. And it's *hot, hot, hot*! The tiniest bit can be tasted in over 700 pounds of mild sauce. Can I have a barrel of icewater with that, please?

137

How come it never SNOWS in some places?

It never gets cold enough. To stay frozen, snowflakes must remain in a cold temperature on their fall to the earth. In some spots, especially those closest to the equator, the climate is always warm. However, even in warm areas, as you go up from the earth's surface, the temperature gets colder and colder. For example, Mount Kilimanjaro, the highest mountain in Africa, is just south of the equator—but its top is covered with snow.

Why do beavers build dams?

They're building a home. The amazing beaver "lodge" is a marvel of animal architecture. Beavers begin by cutting down trees with their sharp front teeth and powerful jaws. They use the tree trunks to build a watertight dam in a pond or lake. The dam is used to decrease the water level and to widen their living space. Then they build a room with rocks and twigs plastered together with mud. There's even a hole in the floor leading to the pond. Inside, beavers sleep and raise families.

WHAT WILL CARS BE LIKE IN THE FUTURE?

They will be your driving partners. Get into the car and say "Good morning," and the seats and mirrors will adjust for you. Tell the car "Sorting mode," and it will get ready to rumble on country roads. If it rains, the windshield wipers will go on automatically. If you're too close to an object, the car will put on its brakes. A car that can help prevent accidents is really something to look forward to.

If your skin is always renewing itself, how can you have a scar for life?

Your skin is like a rug woven of many fibers. If a cut isn't too wide, skin cells reweave the rug just like new. But if the cut edges are far apart, skin cells can't bridge the gap. Fibroblasts, cells that make bigger, tougher strands of skin, fill the space. This becomes a permanent scar.

WHAT'S A SONIC BOOM?

A thunderous noise that occurs when an airplane flies faster than the speed of sound—about 760 miles per hour. When a jet plane breaks through the sound barrier, it presses against the air in front of and beside it. After the jet passes, the air expands again. The air molecules expand so fast that they collide with each other. This collision creates a BOOM and powerful shock waves that could shatter glass.

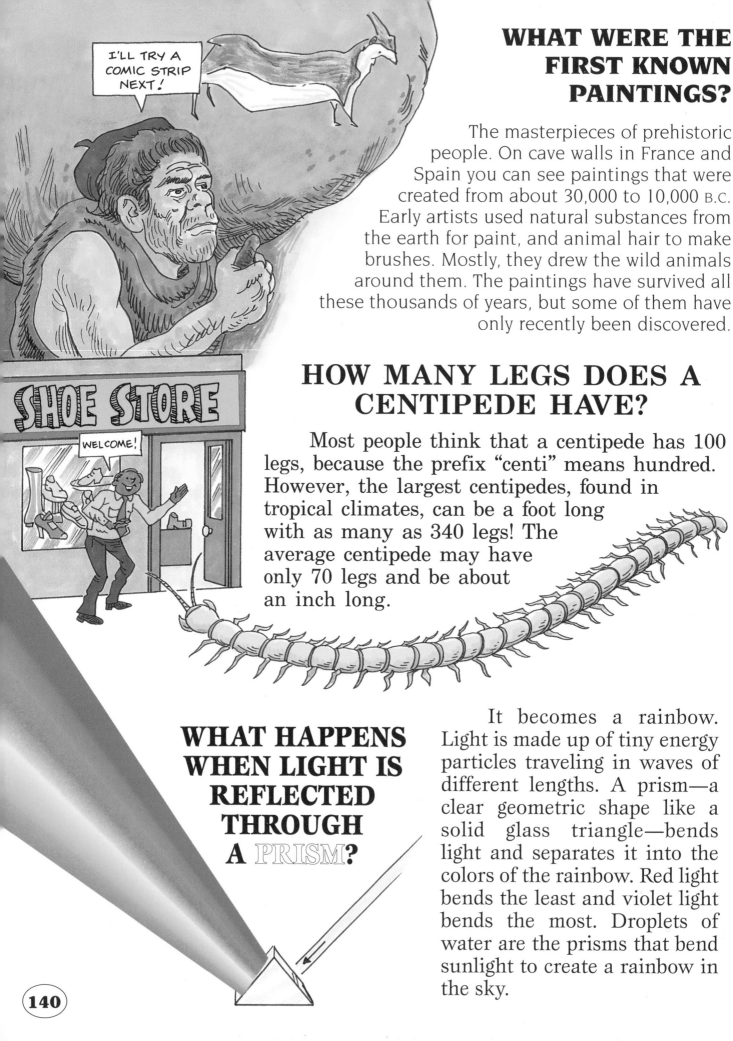

WHAT WERE THE FIRST KNOWN PAINTINGS?

The masterpieces of prehistoric people. On cave walls in France and Spain you can see paintings that were created from about 30,000 to 10,000 B.C. Early artists used natural substances from the earth for paint, and animal hair to make brushes. Mostly, they drew the wild animals around them. The paintings have survived all these thousands of years, but some of them have only recently been discovered.

HOW MANY LEGS DOES A CENTIPEDE HAVE?

Most people think that a centipede has 100 legs, because the prefix "centi" means hundred. However, the largest centipedes, found in tropical climates, can be a foot long with as many as 340 legs! The average centipede may have only 70 legs and be about an inch long.

WHAT HAPPENS WHEN LIGHT IS REFLECTED THROUGH A PRISM?

It becomes a rainbow. Light is made up of tiny energy particles traveling in waves of different lengths. A prism—a clear geometric shape like a solid glass triangle—bends light and separates it into the colors of the rainbow. Red light bends the least and violet light bends the most. Droplets of water are the prisms that bend sunlight to create a rainbow in the sky.

I'LL TRY A COMIC STRIP NEXT!

SHOE STORE

WELCOME!

When were plays first performed?

The earliest known plays were performed in Athens, Greece, around the sixth century B.C. They were part of a spring festival honoring the Greek god Dionysus.

Plays were also performed in ancient Egypt more than 5,000 years ago.

The original video games seem pretty primitive compared to today's screen action. The first video game, invented in the 1970s by Nolan Bushnell, was a screen version of Ping-Pong called "Pong." At first, it was played only in arcades. Bushnell went on to develop Atari, the first successful home video system. Then Pac-Man came chomping along and was a huge success. Today's sophisticated video games, most of which can be played on a computer, are much more challenging and look like cartoons!

HOW CAN WATER CREATE ELECTRICITY?

The force of falling water over a dam can power machines that make electricity. Here's how it works. Water falls from a great height onto the paddles of a turbine—think of a pinwheel spinning when you blow on it. These giant metal turbines whirl up to 750 revolutions per minute. They provide the mechanical energy that rotates the magnet in an electric generator. The generator uses magnets and copper wires to create electrical energy. This electricity travels through wires to the lightbulb on your desk.

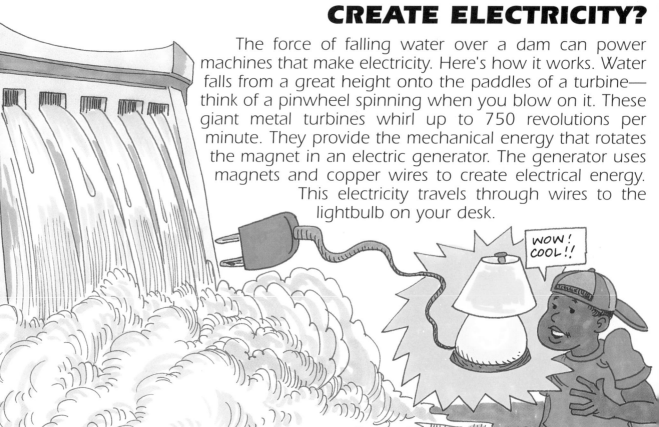

WOW! COOL!!

Are all snakes POISONOUS?

No. Snakes have a bad reputation because of the few poisonous ones. Of the 2,700 snake species, only about 400 are poisonous. Fewer than 50 kinds are dangerous to people. Most snakes will avoid people if at all possible. And most people will avoid snakes! The anaconda, weighing up to 400 pounds, is not poisonous but can squeeze the life out of a crocodile.

YOU RATTLE ME!

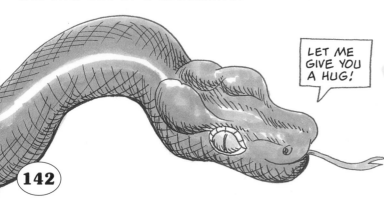

LET ME GIVE YOU A HUG!

WHY DO BABY TEETH FALL OUT?

They need to be replaced by bigger, stronger adult teeth. As you get bigger, your mouth grows. Soon, baby teeth no longer fit. When an adult tooth is ready to come in, it releases a chemical that dissolves the roots of the baby tooth it will replace. Without roots, the tooth is no longer anchored to the jawbone. It loosens and falls out—or gets pulled out!

How did the tooth fairy legend start?

Dr. Rosemary Wells, who's been researching the tooth fairy for more than 20 years, says that losing baby teeth has been important in all cultures, even ancient ones. It's a symbol of "leaving babyhood and entering childhood." Some countries have invented magical animals instead of a fairy. The United States is the only country with a tooth fairy who exchanges money for teeth! Dr. Wells has a Tooth Fairy Museum in Illinois with all kinds of objects, even a singing tooth fairy toothbrush.

WHO WAS THE FIRST WOMAN IN SPACE ?

I'M VALENTINA TERESHKOVA.

I'M SALLY RIDE

In June of 1963, Valentina Tereshkova of the former Soviet Union became the first woman in space. She spent 71 hours aboard Vostok 6. Sally Ride was the first American woman in space. An astrophysicist from California, Sally made her historic journey in 1983.

Why does poison ivy make people itch?

There's no poison in poison ivy, just an oil on the leaf that really clings to the skin. Your skin cells may detect this oil as an enemy. The cells rush to your defense, releasing chemicals that cause your skin to redden and blister, and ooze and itch, while they fight off the invader.

How did the black widow spider get its name?

By her nasty reputation. The black widow is a female spider that often eats the male she mates with! So when she kills her "husband," she becomes a "widow"— and a wicked one at that. Her venom is 15 times stronger than a rattlesnake's!

Basically, your mind works on two levels. The one you are aware of is your thinking, *conscious* mind. The one you aren't aware of is your *subconscious* mind, which stores up memories, dreams, and hidden feelings. A hypnotist guides you to your subconscious mind by helping you become totally relaxed. Most techniques direct you to focus your thoughts on one thing. When you're hypnotized you are not asleep. You can be aware of everything going on around you, but you stay focused. It's a type of concentration similar to daydreaming in class. You get so caught up in your own mind that you don't hear the sounds of your teacher or classmates. Sometimes this state is called a trance.

HOW DOES HYPNOTISM WORK?

WHY DOES JUMBO MEAN BIG?

Jumbo was an elephant who got his name from one of the most famous showmen who ever lived, P.T. Barnum (1810-1891), founder of the Barnum & Bailey Circus. Barnum was a man who knew how to capture an audience. His elephant was big—11 feet tall and 6½ tons—and his catchy name made him so famous that "jumbo" came to mean huge, gigantic, enormous, or just plain large. We can thank Jumbo, who died in 1885, for a very modern phrase—the jumbo jet.

WHAT IS THE WORLD'S TALLEST STATUE?

A 394-foot statue of Buddha in Tokyo, Japan. Buddha, who lived from about 563 to 483 B.C., founded Buddhism, one of the great Asian religions. The bronze statue that honors him is 115 feet wide, and as tall as a 40-story skyscraper. The statue took seven years to build, and was finally completed in 1993.

What is the largest lizard?

A lizard so large it's called a dragon—the Komodo dragon. This very scary creature can be 10 feet long and weigh 300 pounds. Its favorite meal is goat, and it has been known to attack humans. As a matter of fact, the Komodo dragon doesn't even have to bite to cause harm. Its saliva is so deadly that a good spray could do the trick. There are not many Komodo dragons in the world and they all live on a few small islands in Indonesia.

KISS ME!

WHO INVENTED CHOCOLATE CHIP COOKIES?

Thank the cooks at a country inn in Whitman, Massachusetts. Around 1930, they put together a recipe combining bits of chocolate with cookie dough. The cookie was crunchy, buttery, and it tasted like candy, too! The combination is so simple and delicious that it's amazing no one ever thought of it before.

YUM!

YUM!

COOKIE!

ANY AGE LIKES THEM!

GO FOR IT!

Is there anything smaller than an atom?

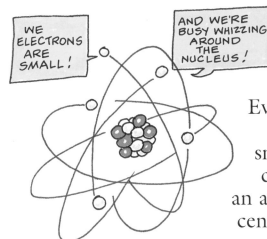

Yes—the particles that make up an atom. Everything is made of atoms, including you and the chair you're sitting on. But they're so small—maybe a millionth of an inch—that they can be seen only with special microscopes. But an atom is made up of still smaller particles. At its center is a nucleus, which is 10,000 times smaller than the rest of the atom. And the nucleus is surrounded by electrons, which are even smaller!

WHAT MAKES MY STOMACH GROWL?

It's telling you it wants food to digest! Digestion happens automatically. When your stomach is empty its muscles still contract, as if it's looking for food. The walls squeeze together, creating the noises you hear. Digestive juices and acids roll around—rumbling, grumbling, and growling.

What is sleepwalking?

Walking in your sleep, without any idea that you're moving. Sleepwalkers commonly perform actions such as looking for lost objects or trying to solve other problems. But we don't know too much more than that. You might think that sleepwalking and dreaming go together, but they don't. Experiments show that sleepwalking occurs during very deep sleep. Dreaming occurs during light sleep.

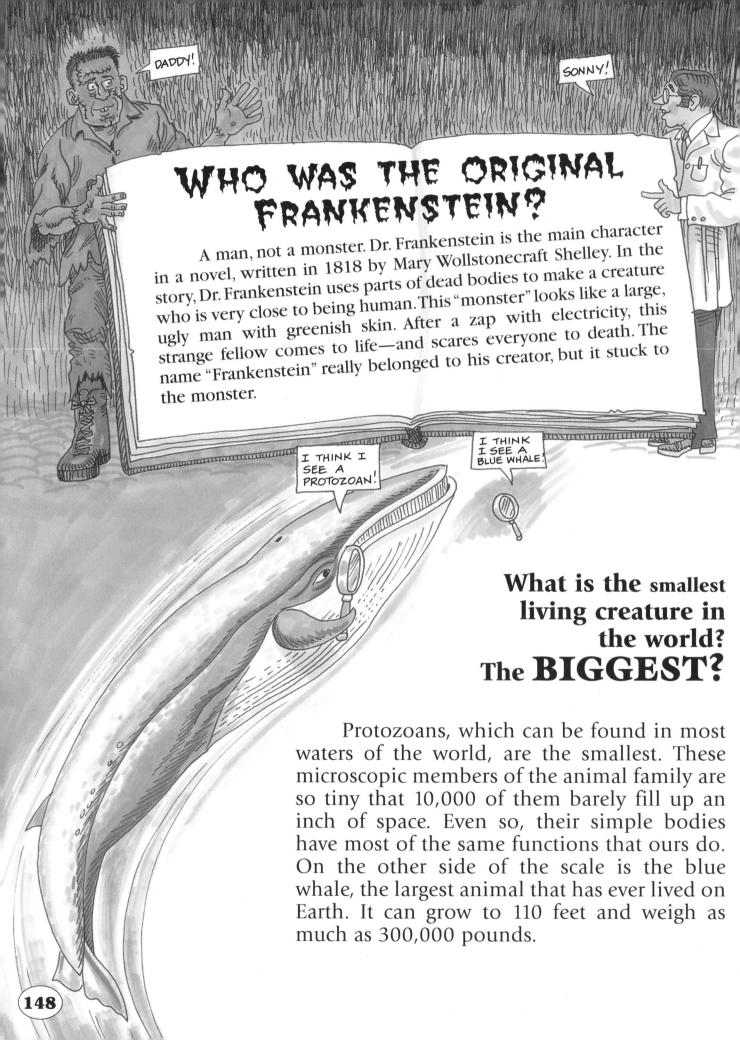

WHO WAS THE ORIGINAL FRANKENSTEIN?

A man, not a monster. Dr. Frankenstein is the main character in a novel, written in 1818 by Mary Wollstonecraft Shelley. In the story, Dr. Frankenstein uses parts of dead bodies to make a creature who is very close to being human. This "monster" looks like a large, ugly man with greenish skin. After a zap with electricity, this strange fellow comes to life—and scares everyone to death. The name "Frankenstein" really belonged to his creator, but it stuck to the monster.

What is the smallest living creature in the world? The BIGGEST?

Protozoans, which can be found in most waters of the world, are the smallest. These microscopic members of the animal family are so tiny that 10,000 of them barely fill up an inch of space. Even so, their simple bodies have most of the same functions that ours do. On the other side of the scale is the blue whale, the largest animal that has ever lived on Earth. It can grow to 110 feet and weigh as much as 300,000 pounds.

How do meteorologists predict the weather?

IT'S A NICE DAY!

They start with the world and then concentrate on your neighborhood.

First, they look at the big picture. Thousands of weather stations around the world measure temperature, humidity, air pressure, and wind direction. Weather balloons and satellites also provide information.

Next, computer programs take all these numbers and predict how world weather conditions are likely to move and change.

Finally, meteorologists consider all these facts and make a good guess about what will happen where you live.

What is D-Day?

D-Day is the code name for the first day of a planned military attack. But World War II gave the name special meaning. During that war, Germany held France. But on D-Day, June 6, 1944, American, British, and other Allied soldiers attacked the Germans on the beaches of Normandy in France. That day was the beginning of the end for Germany, which surrendered less than a year later.

WE'VE LANDED ON OMAHA BEACH!

Why do eyes sometimes look **RED** in photos?

When a camera flash is pointed directly into your eyes, the light travels through your pupils. The camera actually takes a picture of the insides of your eyes. There are so many blood vessels in your eyes that the camera sees red.

What happens when water **FREEZES?**

Ice happens. Temperature affects the way molecules, the microscopic "building blocks" of a substance, bind together. At room temperature, water molecules are loosely connected. That's why water flows. But as the temperature drops to 32°F, water molecules slowly bind together until ice is formed.

HARD WATER!

What was the world's first instrument?

Scientists discovered a piece of animal bone that may have been part of an ancient flute. Amazingly, the holes seem to be spaced in such a way that they play part of the musical scale we know today. Experts guess the bone instrument is 43,000 to 82,000 years old. It was found in a region once inhabited by the Neanderthals, an early human species. So it seems that *do*, *re*, *mi* has been around for a long, long time.

LET'S SIGN HIM UP FOR OUR ROCK BAND!

WHY DO MY EARS POP IN AN AIRPLANE?

CAPTAIN, I JUST HEARD A POP!

It's in the air. Your eardrum is in its normal position when the air pressure is the same inside and outside your ear. When an airplane goes up or down, the air pressure outside the plane changes. The pilot must adjust the pressure inside the plane. This quick change in air pressure may cause a bulge in your eardrum. When the air pressure becomes equal again, your eardrum "pops" back into place.

How many people have lived in the world since humans came to exist?

About fifty billion is the best guess, and the number is increasing. Every minute, approximately 160 babies are born around the world.

Where did bullfighting begin?

Even though bullfighting was known 4,000 years ago on the Greek island of Crete, Spain is the name to know when it comes to bulls and fighting. The Moors, Arabs who once ruled Spain, began the sport in the 11th century. Today bullfighting is still popular in Spain, Portugal, Mexico, and parts of South America.

THAT'S A LOT OF BULL!

IT'S MINE... ALL MINE!!

Who was Genghis Khan?

A man with a plan to conquer the whole world. Genghis Khan (1167–1227), originally named Temüjin, was a Mongolian leader who came to power at only 13 years of age. The young ruler soon became known as Genghis Khan—"precious warrior." He united the Mongol tribes into a fierce fighting force. They invaded what is now China, Russia, Iran, and northwest India, creating one of the greatest empires of all time. Upon Genghis Khan's death, the Mongol Empire was divided among his three sons and gradually dissolved.

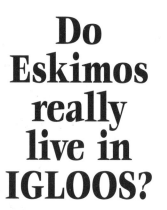

MUST SELL BEFORE SUMMER

Do Eskimos really live in IGLOOS?

Not anymore. Igloos, or snow houses, were once used by Eskimos as temporary shelter when they traveled. Blocks of hard-packed snow or ice, about three feet long and two feet wide, were stacked in circles to form a dome-shaped house. Cozy on the inside, igloos were lit and heated by lamps that burned oil made from the blubber of sea mammals.

Why do monkeys and apes groom each other?

Why do humans shake hands or give hugs? Touching is a form of communication. A social act, grooming helps to keep a group of monkeys together. Grooming is also symbolic of a monkey's social status. A monkey grooms those with a higher social position and is groomed by those of lower rank. Above all, grooming keeps monkeys clean!

What is the Concorde?

WAIT FOR ME!!

The fastest way to travel. Instead of seven hours in the air from New York to Paris, the Concorde can get you there in three! The Concorde is the first supersonic passenger jet. It travels at more than 1,000 miles an hour. A British-French partnership put the plane into service in 1976. However, there aren't many Concordes flying around. This type of plane is still too expensive to make and keep up!

What would happen if there were no more plants in the world?

ULP!

Not much could happen. Plants are a necessary link in the cycle of nature that connects all living things. *Photosynthesis*, the process by which plants use sunlight to make their own food, supplies us with the oxygen we breathe. Plants are a source of food and shelter for many animals. Plants also keep the soil from blowing away in the wind. There would be no world as we know it without plants.

Do stars last forever?

No. Stars are mostly made up of hydrogen gas, which they are constantly burning. That's why stars shine. Eventually, they burn themselves up and explode, or simply burn out. How long that takes depends on the star. Giant stars, bigger than our sun, actually burn out quicker than smaller stars. Scientists believe our sun has been burning for five billion years—and it has five billion more to go. That's a long time, but it's not forever.

WHO HAS WON THE MOST OLYMPIC MEDALS?

I WISH I COULD DO THAT!

Larissa Latynina, a gymnast from the former Soviet Union, won 18 Olympic medals in all—9 gold, 5 silver, and 4 bronze. That's the most medals for an athlete in any sport. Amazingly, she did it in just 3 years—1956, 1960, and 1964. The women gymnastics stars that followed made the sport popular, but Larissa started it all.

HOW DOES SOMETHING BECOME RADIOACTIVE?

HERE I COME!

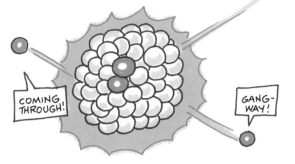

COMING THROUGH!

GANG-WAY!

Atoms are the tiny "building blocks" of all substances. Atoms contain energy. Over time, the *nucleus*, or center, of every atom decays. When this happens, parts of the atom shoot out in high-energy rays. This is called nuclear radiation, or radioactivity. When something is radioactive it becomes electrically charged. Most radioactive rays are too weak to harm us, but strong rays can be dangerous. Radioactivity is helpful for scientists who do medical research or study the Earth.

What is the most common name on the planet?

For centuries, Mary was the most common girl's name worldwide. It's no longer the most common, but no other girl's name has strongly replaced it. Mohammed is the most common boy's name.

HARRY
MANNY
DOTTIE
MARY
ANTHONY
WANDA
ELVIRA
MAX
NINA
MICHAEL
MARIA
JOSE
TRACY
STACY
DAN
CHRIS
HARRIET

154

How much BLOOD is in my body?

HE USED HIS NOODLE!

WHO CREATED SPAGHETTI?

The legend says that Italian explorer Marco Polo brought spaghetti back from China in 1292. However, carvings in a 5,000-year-old tomb near Rome show all the tools needed to make pasta. So who did it first—China or Italy? We may never know, but there is general agreement that Naples, Italy, is the birthplace of spaghetti as we know it today.

DID SOMEBODY SAY *BLOOD*?

I'D RATHER HAVE PASTA!

VENICE

CHINA

A grown-up has about 5 quarts of blood in his or her body. That means you probably have about 3 or 4 quarts of blood in your body. There are 4 quarts in a gallon. To get an idea of how much that is, think of one big container of milk.

WHO INVENTED THE JIGSAW PUZZLE?

An Englishman who wanted to teach a geography lesson. In 1767, John Silsbury carved a wooden map of England and divided it into counties. Each county was one piece. They fit around each other according to their location. Puzzles as we know them today were developed in the 20th century.

I'M FAMOUS!

What is PLASTIC made of?

STRING

HAMMER

DAMPER

How does a PIANO make sound when you press a key?

Each of a piano's 88 keys is attached to at least one steel wire string. Each string has a "hammer" that strikes it. Pressing a key causes the hammer to strike its string. When the string is struck, it vibrates and makes the sound you think of as a "note." All together, there are nearly 4,000 parts in the action of one piano. And with only ten fingers, you can make all this action happen.

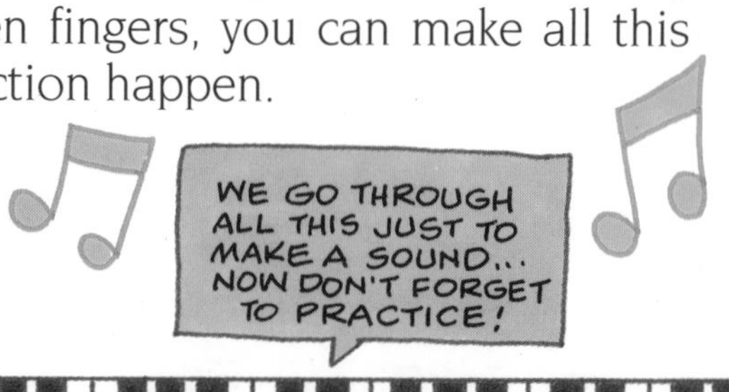

KEY

WE GO THROUGH ALL THIS JUST TO MAKE A SOUND... NOW DON'T FORGET TO PRACTICE!

Where is the Great Barrier Reef?

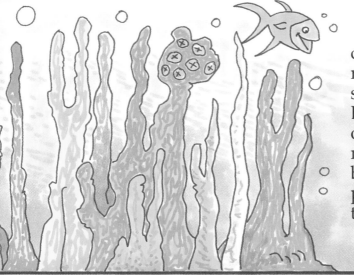

It stretches along the northeast coast of Australia—for 1,250 miles! A reef is a ridge in the ocean close to the surface of the water. The Great Barrier Reef, made up of the remains of tiny sea creatures, is a chain of more than 2,500 reefs. Billions and billions of coral skeletons have been piling up for nearly 15 million years to form the largest reef in the world.

Mixed-up oil molecules. Scientists discovered plastic by rearranging some of the molecules in oil. The process is called *polymerization*. Many *synthetic* (human-made) substances are created this way, including different kinds of plastic. The first useful plastic was celluloid, invented in 1870 by John Hyatt. It was used to make billiard balls. Maybe he liked to shoot pool!

WHAT IS SPELUNKING?

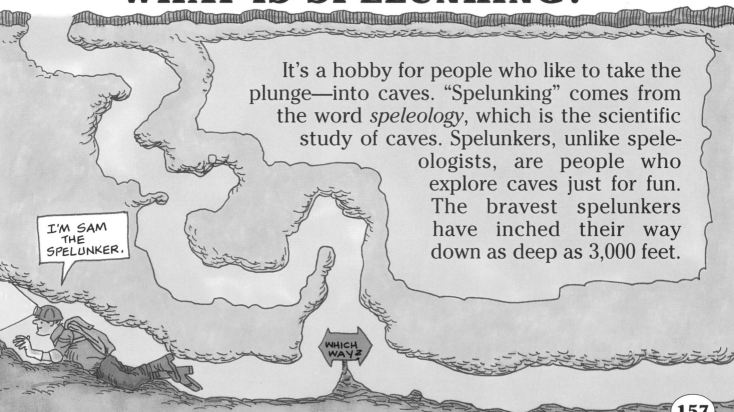

It's a hobby for people who like to take the plunge—into caves. "Spelunking" comes from the word *speleology*, which is the scientific study of caves. Spelunkers, unlike speleologists, are people who explore caves just for fun. The bravest spelunkers have inched their way down as deep as 3,000 feet.

I'M SAM THE SPELUNKER.

WHICH WAY?

Who was AMELIA EARHART?

A daring pilot with a mysterious death. Earhart (1897-1937) was the first woman to fly solo across the Atlantic ocean—but that's not all. She also made the first solo flight from Hawaii to the United States mainland, and she was also the first woman to fly nonstop across the United States. But she never completed her flight around the world. During that voyage in 1937, Earhart's plane disappeared over the Pacific Ocean—and not a trace was ever found.

HOW DOES A FAX MACHINE KNOW WHAT TO PRINT?

Electricity is used by the fax machine to "see" what it's printing. Fax is short for facsimile, which means a copy. When you send a fax, you send a copy of words or pictures to a fax machine at another location. A scanner in the fax machine "reads" the images by coding the dark areas in electrical signals. The signals travel over telephone wires. Finally, the printer in the receiving machine prints out the dark pattern in tiny dots, just the way your machine sent them.

Why is it easier to balance on my bicycle when it's moving than when it's standing still?

A spinning wheel will stay upright on its own. This motion is called *precession*. You've seen it in a spinning top. The faster it spins, the longer the top stays up. As the spinning slows down, the top begins to wobble. The same goes for a bicycle wheel. The faster it spins, the more likely it is to stay up—and so are you!

THAT'S GREAT... BUT, I'M LOST!

How does a thermometer work?

Heat and the metal mercury work together in a glass thermometer. A thermometer is a thin tube of glass with a hollow bulb at one end. The bulb is filled with mercury. When the mercury is heated, it expands and moves up the tube. The distance it moves is measured in degrees.

IT'S HOT TODAY!

C F
100 210

NORTH POLE

What are the Northern and Southern Lights?

A heavenly display of light and color in the night sky. Near the North and South Poles, electrical particles from the sun are entrapped by Earth's magnetic field. These particles strike molecules in Earth's atmosphere. The collision causes the molecules to glow, creating an *aurora*. The Northern Lights are called *aurora borealis* and the Southern Lights *aurora australis*. Both occur at the same time, and both are unforgettable.

HOW LARGE WAS THE LARGEST CAKE EVER BAKED?

128,238 pounds, 8 ounces. The icing alone weighed 16,209 pounds! The cake was in the shape of Alabama, baked to celebrate the 100th birthday of Fort Payne, a town with a gigantic taste for sweets.

A MASTERPIECE

WOW!

LOOKS DELICIOUS.

ARF! (YUM!)

Why do we itch? Does scratching

an itch?

Itching and scratching seem simple, but they're mysterious. Scientists don't know exactly how to explain itching. We do know that certain sensations cause us to itch. For example, if an ant marched across your foot, it would itch. To stop the itching you would scratch. Scratching is a much more powerful sensation, so the itch seems to go away.

What do Mars and Venus look like?

VENUS — I'M HOT!

EARTH — I'M JUST RIGHT.

THE MOON — I'M HOT AND COLD!

MARS — I'M COLD.

Mars is named for the Roman god of war because it looks bloodred. When space scientists took a closer look, they realized that the color is caused by rusted iron in the soil. The surface of Mars is covered by rocks and mountains. *Olympus Mons*, 16 miles high, is the tallest mountain in our solar system.

The rocky surface of Venus has large craters and high mountains. But the surface is difficult to see because the planet is surrounded by thick clouds. The clouds reflect and absorb sunlight, making Venus the hottest planet—over 800°F—and one of the brightest in our solar system.

What are CRYSTALS made of?

Minerals are the basic elements of crystals. Crystals form when molten minerals, or minerals dissolved in heated liquid, cool. Each type of mineral forms crystals with particular shapes. For example, the mineral *galena*, the main source of lead, forms four-sided cubic crystals. Even though crystals are nonliving substances, they can "grow," or increase, by forming the same link over and over. This process is called *crystallization*.

Who invented LANGUAGE?

No one knows for sure because there are certainly no written records of how words developed! Scholars think language may have begun around 3000 B.C., because the Sumerians of the Middle East invented writing around that time. This early form of writing, called *cuneiform* (kyu-NEE-uh-form), used symbols for whole words. The alphabet was invented in the Middle East around 1500 B.C. by the Phoenicians.

PUT ME DOWN MOM!

Why doesn't it hurt a kitten when its mother picks it up by the scruff of its neck?

Kittens have plenty of loose skin around their neck, so the mother can get a good grip without pulling too hard. She hangs on to the skin but is careful not to bite. The kitten also cooperates by staying still. That way it's an easy, painless ride.

SOB! I'M NOT REAL! SOB!

DO VAMPIRES REALLY EXIST?

Of course not! Vampires were made up by good storytellers. Still, the idea of a body rising from the grave to suck your blood is so horrible, some people are scared into believing vampires exist. According to legend, sleeping with garlic around your neck or putting salt on your windowsill ought to keep vampires away.

Who are some of the most famous women leaders?

GOOD SHOW, MAGGIE!

CLEOPATRA

#1

MARGARET THATCHER

Women have held great power ever since Queen Hatshepsut ruled ancient Egypt around 1400 B.C. Cleopatra took the same role in 51 B.C. One of the most famous monarchs in history was Catherine the Great, Empress of Russia (1729-1796). Queen Victoria ruled the British Empire for more than 50 years. The 20th century has seen many more women leaders, including Indira Gandhi of India, Golda Meir as Prime Minister of Israel, and Margaret Thatcher, the first female Prime Minister of Great Britain.

What's the difference between honeybees and wasps?

IF I STING YOU... I'M HISTORY!!

I HATE THE WINTER!

They belong to the same family, *Apoidea*, but there are many differences. Honeybees live in hives. Some wasps build a nest out of "paper," which they make by chewing on wood and passing it through their body. Another difference is that honeybees collect the sweet nectar from flowers to make honey. Wasps make a meal of other insects. Also, if a honeybee stings, it loses its stinger and dies. Not the wasp. It stings and lives to sting again. But honeybees live through the winter. Wasps, alas, do not.

Where is the longest river in the world? The deepest lake?

NILE RIVER

I LIVE HERE.

The Nile River, running through Egypt and Sudan in Africa, is the longest river in the world. It's about 4,160 miles long. The Amazon River, running through South America, comes close at about 4,000 miles. Siberia, in Russia, is home to the deepest lake, Lake Baykal. Its lowest point plunges more than a mile below the surface— 5,315 feet.

HOW DOES A GLACIER FORM?

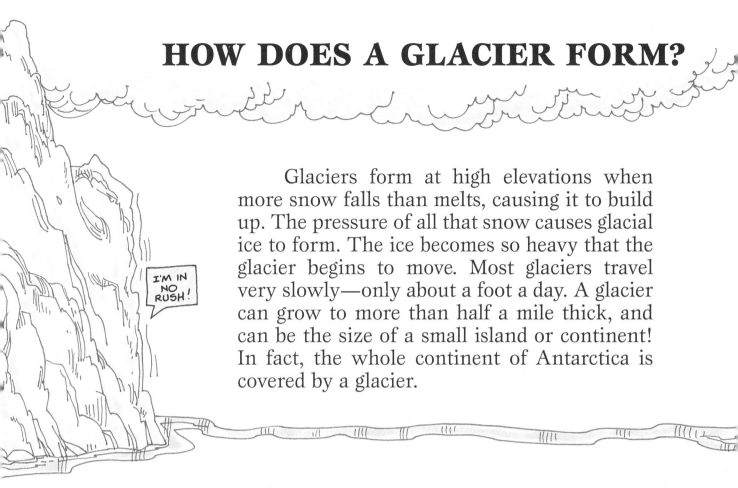

I'M IN NO RUSH!

Glaciers form at high elevations when more snow falls than melts, causing it to build up. The pressure of all that snow causes glacial ice to form. The ice becomes so heavy that the glacier begins to move. Most glaciers travel very slowly—only about a foot a day. A glacier can grow to more than half a mile thick, and can be the size of a small island or continent! In fact, the whole continent of Antarctica is covered by a glacier.

HOW DOES A CAMERA WORK?

EVERYONE THAT'S LOOKING AT THIS PAGE SMILE!

In the blink of an eye. A camera works very quickly. Light only hits the film for a fraction of a second. The film, which records the picture, is very "light sensitive." When you take a picture, you look through the *view finder* and aim the camera. You press the button. The *shutter*, an opening and closing device, opens to let light in. The *lens* directs the light onto the film. Instantly, the shutter closes. Whatever the camera "saw" in that brief moment is what you get.

What is the ozone layer?

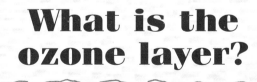

It's part of Earth's atmosphere. As you go up from the ground, the gases that make up the atmosphere change. These "layers" of gas have different names. The ozone layer is about 12 to 30 miles above Earth's surface. Ozone is a form of oxygen that absorbs much of the sun's ultraviolet radiation and prevents it from reaching the ground. If this radiation did reach ground level, it would be harmful to most forms of life.

How does water get to my sink?

It starts in a natural source like a lake, river, or reservoir. The water is pumped through pipes into large tanks. Fish, plants, and trash are screened out. Chemicals like chlorine are added to kill any bacteria or dangerous substances. If you live in a city, the water is then pumped into cast iron pipes called mains. The mains run beneath the streets and carry water to every hydrant, house, and building. The pumping station sends the water to every faucet. If you live in a rural area, water is pumped from a well right into your house. Turn it on!

WHAT IS A BRUISE?

A bruise is a bunch of broken blood vessels beneath the skin. When they break, blood oozes out into the tissues around the spot. The tissues turn a purplish color. As the bruise heals, it changes into a rainbow of colors—first blue, then green, and finally yellow before it disappears. This happens as the blood is absorbed into the body again.

Why do people eat turkey on Thanksgiving?

It has become a tradition. The first Thanksgiving in the New World was a celebration by the Pilgrims in 1621. It was an effort to thank the Native Americans who had helped the Pilgrims survive their first year. Our only real clue that they ate turkey is in a letter written by one of the men. It said the governor sent four men "fowling" for the feast. A turkey is a fowl—and there were plenty of wild turkeys roaming the woods in Massachusetts. Also, since Massasoit, the Indian chief, brought 90 braves for dinner, fat turkeys would have been very useful. By the early 1800s turkey became the Thanksgiving bird of America.

What is the Nobel Prize?

Annual awards given to people around the world who make "contributions to the good of humanity." Alfred Bernhard Nobel (1833-1896) was a Swedish chemist who invented dynamite and became extremely rich. He never got over the destruction his invention caused. Before he died, Nobel established a fund for prizes in physics, chemistry, medicine, literature, economics, and peace.

WHAT ANIMAL HAS TEETH ALL OVER ITS BODY?

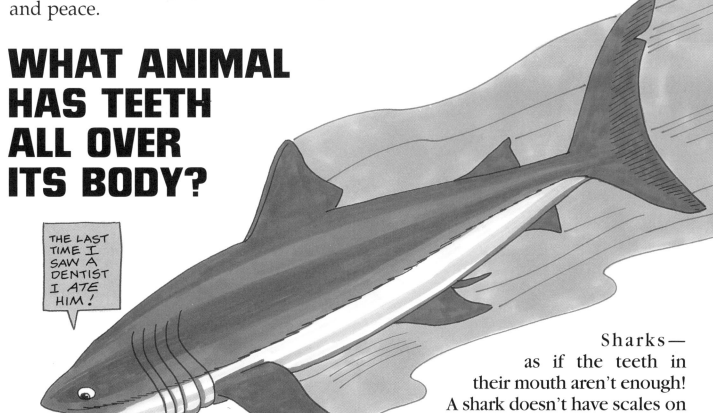

Sharks—as if the teeth in their mouth aren't enough! A shark doesn't have scales on its body like other fish. Most sharks have *denticles* instead. A shark's body is covered with these small, razor-sharp, toothlike constructions. Denticles overlap like scales, but if you rubbed up against them, they would rip right through your skin!

What happened during the GOLD RUSH?

During the 1800s in North America there were several gold discoveries. As soon as someone discovered gold, people "rushed" to the spot hoping to get rich. California, Colorado, and Alaska are the most famous gold-digging spots. In 1848, gold was found near a small town called San Francisco. A year later, 25,000 people lived there. In just one more year, there were so many miners in the territory that California had enough people to become a state.

Where is the world's BIGGEST gingerbread house?

It was in Iowa, a state more famous for corn than gingerbread. In December of 1988, 100 people put together 2,000 sheets of gingerbread and 1,650 pounds of frosting. Their masterpiece was as tall as a five-story house—52 feet high—until everyone ate it!

How does an egg hatch?

It's all in the tooth—the egg tooth. Both baby birds and reptiles chip their way out of a shell with a small, sharp tooth. A bird's egg tooth grows on its beak. A snake's is on its upper jaw. After the work of hatching is done, the egg tooth falls away.

Who built the GIGANTIC statues on Easter Island and why?

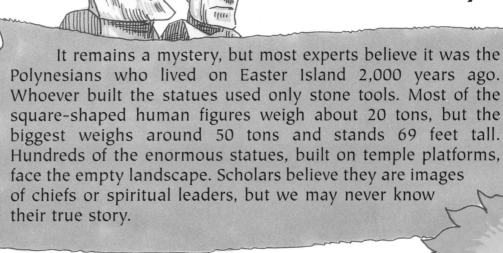

It remains a mystery, but most experts believe it was the Polynesians who lived on Easter Island 2,000 years ago. Whoever built the statues used only stone tools. Most of the square-shaped human figures weigh about 20 tons, but the biggest weighs around 50 tons and stands 69 feet tall. Hundreds of the enormous statues, built on temple platforms, face the empty landscape. Scholars believe they are images of chiefs or spiritual leaders, but we may never know their true story.

WHY IS IT HOTTER NEAR THE EQUATOR?

The equator is the great imaginary line that circles Earth halfway between the North and South Poles. It's this location that makes the equator such a hot spot. Because the Earth is curved, the most direct sunlight rays strike at the equator. The least direct sunlight hits the poles. But in Ecuador, a country on the equator, the city of Quito has a very high elevation. The altitude cools the temperature down to an average of about 58°F.

What is the world's most popular spectator sport?

OUCH!

Soccer, which has been popular for quite a while. A ball made of animal skins may have been kicked around in ancient China. But other countries want to take credit for soccer, including Japan, Mexico, and Greece. Native Americans played a game in the 1600s called *pasuckuakohowog*, which means "they gather to play ball with the foot." The English finally set down regular rules for the game in 1863. Today, soccer is played in 140 nations and the whole world watches it!

WHY DO FLEAS LIVE ON CATS AND DOGS?

I'M MOVING!

Your pets are the fleas' dinner. Warm-blooded animals such as cats, dogs, squirrels, birds, and even humans are all on the flea menu. Blood is what fleas are after. Fleas can be controlled with certain kinds of chemicals called insecticides, as well as ordinary soap! Believe it or not, staying clean helps make your pet unfit for fleas to grow on. A flea collar coated with chemicals helps, too!

What animal has eyes at the end of its arms, and feet under its arms?

ION.

The starfish. The "sea star" (its real name) is not necessarily a star and not a fish at all. It's a creature that lives in the ocean and takes several shapes. The most common is the five-pointed star—five "arms" with a body in the center.

The sea star "sees" with a small colored eye-spot at the tip of each arm. These eyespots sense light but can't form images. The feet are rows of slender tubes that extend from the body to the end of each arm. With a suction disk at each tip, the sea star crawls along the ocean floor.

WHERE WAS THE WORLD'S BIGGEST FIREWORKS DISPLAY?

It was not for the Fourth of July. The big bang was in Hokkaido, Japan in 1988 at the Lake Toya Festival. The flash and light started with a 1,543-pound shell that exploded, lighting the sky in a giant circle of fireworks that covered almost a mile!

How is a bridge made?

Very carefully! The idea behind all bridges is to build a structure that shifts its weight to places where it can be supported. There are four main types of bridges.

Beam bridge: A flat road goes across a short, shallow river. It's held up by a long line of straight piers (supports) placed in the river floor.

Arch bridge: The road is placed over one or more arches built over the river. The weight of the road creates pressure that shifts down each side of the bridge to the "feet" anchored in the earth.

Cantilever bridge: There are two sections, one on each side of the river. The balance between the two sides supports a road between them.

WE ALL HAVE TOLLS!

Suspension bridge: The road is hung from giant, thick steel cables. These anchored cables shift the road's weight to the ground. One of the best-known suspension bridges is the Golden Gate Bridge in San Francisco, California.

What is NASA?

The National Aeronautics and Space Administration. NASA is an organization in the United States that manages the development and operation of aircrafts in space. It all began in 1958 and has included everything from the first manned flight, to landing on the moon, to satellites that explore other planets, to space shuttles and space stations. Most NASA flights take off from the Kennedy Space Center in Cape Canaveral, Florida. NASA's "command center" is in Houston, Texas.

169

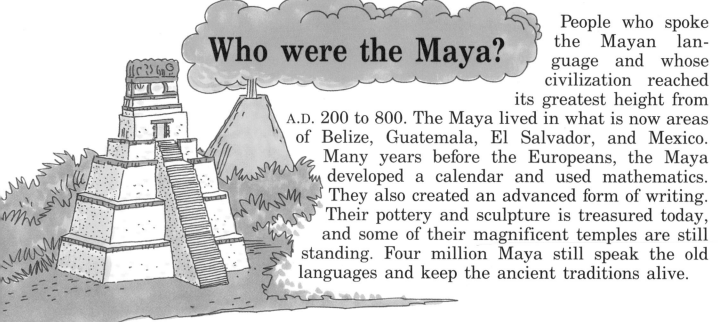

Who were the Maya?

People who spoke the Mayan language and whose civilization reached its greatest height from A.D. 200 to 800. The Maya lived in what is now areas of Belize, Guatemala, El Salvador, and Mexico. Many years before the Europeans, the Maya developed a calendar and used mathematics. They also created an advanced form of writing. Their pottery and sculpture is treasured today, and some of their magnificent temples are still standing. Four million Maya still speak the old languages and keep the ancient traditions alive.

WHAT IS SOLAR HEATING?

Sun power, which creates a great deal of heat. But it's difficult to capture the heat, store it, and use it when you need it. Solar heating is an effort to do just that. Special plates installed on the roof of a house absorb heat from the sun. Once absorbed, the heat is stored in water or rocks in a large container. A heating system circulates the heat throughout the house. Even experimental solar-powered cars have been built!

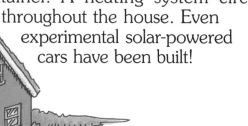

HOW BIG WAS THE WORLD'S BIGGEST SNOWMAN?

If you were on the top floor of a six-story building and stuck your head out the window, you could be nose to nose with the world's biggest snowman. In Alaska, in 1988, a group of people who probably like cold weather spent two weeks building "Super Frosty." When they were done, Frosty the Snowman had a 62-foot-high big brother!

WHY DOES THE MOON LOOK LIKE SWISS CHEESE?

Swiss cheese has holes. The moon has craters, or pits, in the surface. Some of the craters are small, but others are huge—up to 155 miles across—and can be seen from Earth. Most of the craters were made during early periods of the solar system, when space was a traffic jam of rocks and metal flying off the planets as they formed. When these fragments crashed into the moon, the impact caused craters.

Why do babies cry?

To communicate. Babies can't say "I'm so hungry I could eat a horse" or "Get me out of this car seat." So they make the only noise they can—crying. If you're around a baby, you can tell the difference between crying that means hungry, angry, tired, or scared.

Where does the word "Eureka" come from?

Greece. Archimedes (287-212 B.C.) was a Greek mathematician and inventor. The story is that he had just stepped into one of the public baths when an idea came to him. He was so excited that he rushed home yelling "Eureka! Eureka!" (I have found it! I have found it!) So when you discover something you've been looking for, shout "Eureka!"

WHAT IS A MARSUPIAL?

Kangaroos are the most famous marsupials, but some others are opossums, koalas, and wombats. What makes them different from other animals is the "pouch" just below their stomach. The pouch is for carrying their offspring.

Marsupial babies do more of their growing outside the mother's body than inside. At birth, they are very underdeveloped and less than an inch long. These tiny creatures struggle up through their mother's fur and crawl into her pouch. Inside they find nipples for milk and a safe place to hide. A baby kangaroo stays there for five to ten months.

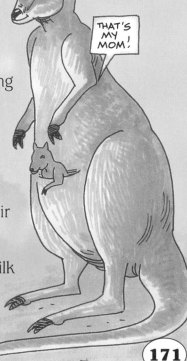

THAT'S MY MOM!

171

Who was Gandhi?

Mohandas Gandhi (1869-1948) guided India to independence from Britain. Called the *Mahatma*, meaning "great soul," Gandhi believed in nonviolence, courage, and truth. At times, he fasted to show belief in his cause. In 1948, one year after India was granted independence, conflicts broke out between Muslims and Hindus. Gandhi encouraged them to live peacefully, and was killed by a Hindu who disagreed with him.

I'M HUNGRY!

HOW DOES A CLAM EAT?

It opens its shell slightly to let dinner in. Tiny hairs filter food into a small mouth, then into the stomach. The food is digested there and absorbed into the intestines. Clams eat tiny water plants and sea animals called plankton. Although clams seem to be bloblike creatures, they have a digestive system, and even a heart and blood vessels.

HOW DOES MY VOICE WORK?

It's all in your vocal cords, a pair of muscles in your windpipe. When air from your lungs passes over your vocal cords, they vibrate. To make sounds, your vocal cords need to contract, or tighten, rather than relax. You control that. The more your vocal cords contract, the more high-pitched the sound.

Your mouth and tongue form these sounds into words.

Why does the word "LOVE" mean ZERO POINTS in tennis?

It certainly doesn't mean tennis players love to lose! The answer is hidden between two languages. Tennis began in France in the 1100s or 1200s. "Love" may have come from the French word *l'oeuf*, which was slang for zero. The English, who invented the modern version of tennis in the late 1800s, pronounced it "luff." Eventually, it became love.

WHO INVENTED PLAYING CARDS?

MY MUMMY TAUGHT ME HOW TO PLAY CARDS.

History has hidden the answer. People must have been too busy playing to stop and say, "Hey, who made up this game?" Most scholars believe that some form of cards began in India and developed in Egypt in the 12th and 13th centuries. By 1380, cards were known in Italy, Switzerland, France, and Spain. In 1452, playing cards were burned in bonfires as a reaction to gambling.

What is the Venus flytrap?

The Venus flytrap is one of 500 types of *carnivorous*, or meat-eating, plants. The plant eats mostly insects though, so don't worry. The two-sided leaves of the Venus are the "fly trap." Each is lined with toothlike spines. When an insect flies inside and touches the trigger hairs...SNAP! The two sides of the leaf clamp together. The insect is caught and slowly digested (it takes about 10 days). Finally, the leaf opens again. After two or three catches, the leaves die and are replaced by younger, snappier leaves.

LUNCH TIME!

173

WHAT IS A WINDMILL USED FOR?

Windmills use the force of the wind to produce power. Wind whips through the blades, which are attached to a shaft. The shaft, which runs down the tower, is connected to an underground pump or mechanical gears. Windmills are used for such tasks as milling grain, pumping water for farmland, pressing oil from seeds, and grinding different materials. Wind turbine generators use the power of the wind to generate electricity. They have huge, propellerlike blades.

What was the PONY EXPRESS?

Eighty mailmen on horseback. The pony express was a well organized mail-delivery system that operated between Missouri and California. In the 1860s, it took teamwork to get mail to its destination. Riders galloped at full speed, stopping at stations every ten miles or so to change horses. Each rider traveled up to 100 miles of the total route—1,966 miles. They hauled the mail in pouches, carrying two guns and a knife to protect themselves against bandits. The whole trip was made in about eight or nine days. One of the riders was 14-year-old William Cody, later known as Buffalo Bill.

How are fossils formed? Where are they found?

When an animal or plant dies, it decays over time. Sometimes, if conditions are right, the earth preserves traces of the animal or plant—for millions of years! Imagine an ancient reptile that died in mud. Its flesh would decay. The bones would slowly dissolve, but minerals might fill in the spaces, harden, and preserve the shape of the bones. That's called a *petrified* fossil. A *mold* fossil is created when an animal or plant dies and its shape forms an impression in the earth. Fossils are found all over the world in places where ancient rocks have been uncovered.

I WAS IN AN ACCIDENT.

DO INSECTS HAVE A HEART AND BLOOD?

Yes—tiny as they may be, insects have pretty complicated working parts. Their heart is a long tube that runs along the top of the body. It pumps blood, which brings digested food to the organs and takes away waste materials. But the blood doesn't carry oxygen, so it isn't red like ours. It's (yuck!) green or blue.

Why is a black cat considered unlucky?

I AM?!

If you fear a black cat crossing your path, blame it on witches. Witchcraft has been around since ancient times. At one time, people believed that each witch had an assistant, or personal demon, called a familiar. Familiars took the form of animals—and many were black cats.

THAT'S MY PET CAT,

Why does Saturn have rings around it?

The planet is surrounded by chunks of ice, plus some dust and metal materials. These particles orbit around Saturn like satellites. Also orbiting Saturn are small *moonlets*, celestial bodies with their own gravitational pull. Scientists believe that the pull of these moonlets keeps the particles together, forming the rings. The rings whirl around Saturn, shining with light coming from the sun.

How are animals trained?

Most animals learn by a method called *operant conditioning*. Basically, each time an animal performs a behavior the trainer has in mind, it receives a reward. The reward is called a *reinforcer* because it reinforces, or encourages, the behavior. Animals don't "think" as we do, but they can learn behaviors in this way. Gorillas, chimpanzees, and marine mammals are trained by this method.

Who was SACAJAWEA?

A Native American woman, of the Shoshone tribe, who made an important contribution to the exploration of America. In 1804, explorers Meriwether Lewis and William Clark set out from St. Louis to find a route to the west coast. Sacajawea went with them as a guide. Their journey would have been much harder without her. She saved them weeks of travel time because she knew the territory and the mountain passes. She found food when it was scarce by gathering wild plants. Lewis and Clark were so grateful, they named a river, a mountain peak, and a mountain pass in her honor.

Does a rain dance work?

If it did, we would have rain whenever our rivers run dry or when crops need water. Many ancient cultures believed that the important forces of nature, like the sun, the earth, and the rain, were gods. It was their way of explaining how the universe worked. To them, it made sense to pray to the god of rain if rain were needed. Many of the songs and dances in these rituals were very beautiful.

WHEN WERE FORKS INVENTED ?

The first forks probably had two prongs and were used to hold meat over a fire. It wasn't until the 1500s in Italy that forks were used at the table, and then only by people who cared enough to keep their shirtsleeves out of their food. Still, forks weren't very common. If you think about it, most foods can be eaten without a fork—but it's hard to eat soup without a spoon!

WHAT'S THE OLDEST INSECT?

The cockroach! Those pesky pests have been around for 350 million years, and they look pretty much the same now as they did then. They have flat bodies, long legs, and range from about one-quarter inch to three inches long. What incredible survivors!

I'VE BEEN AROUND!

How FAST can a cheetah run?

Seventy miles an hour in 25-foot leaps. When it comes to short distances, the cheetah is the fastest land animal on earth. The cat's flexible spine is the secret to its speed. The spine curls and uncurls like elastic, springing the cheetah forward. Speedier than a sports car, the cat bursts from zero to 40 miles per hour in two seconds!

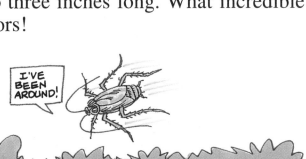

I GOT A TICKET FOR SPEEDING!

SPEEDING TICKET - 40 MPH IN A 20 MPH ZONE

WHY DO I GET THIRSTY?

Your body is trying to tell you something. It's saying you don't have enough water in your bloodstream. Strangely, people who are dehydrated (seriously lacking water) tend to drink just what they need. Scientists think we must have a "water meter" in our bodies, but they haven't found it yet. Salty food also makes us thirsty because salt absorbs water. When you drink enough water to satisfy your body, your thirst is quenched!

ANCHOVY PIZZA MAKES ME THIRSTY!!

WHAT'S THE DIFFERENCE BETWEEN THE ARCTIC AND THE ANTARCTIC?

IT'S A WHALE OF A PLACE!

NORTH POLE

The Arctic is home of the North Pole. The Arctic Circle, an imaginary line 1,630 miles below the Pole, marks the entire region—including the Arctic Ocean, many islands, and northern parts of Europe, Asia, and North America. It's very cold in the Arctic, but in some areas the snow disappears in the summer. The Arctic is home to polar bears, seals, whales, musk oxen, caribou, and birds.

The Antarctic is home of the South Pole. The region covers over five million square miles. At its greatest distance, the icy continent of Antarctica is 3,250 miles across. A few mosses and just two flowering plants manage to survive—along with a small, wingless fly. The Antarctic Ocean is home to fish, birds, seals, whales, and penguins.

SOUTH POLE

IT'S A WHALE OF A PLACE!

What is a werewolf?

I NEED A SHAVE!

A mythical person who changes into a wolf and back into a human again—if you believe it. Werewolves appear in many myths and stories. They are not the type of animal you'd want for a pet. Generally, they bite people and they aren't too cute. Evil or magic power is said to lurk around them. In some cultures, legends claim that people turn into tigers, foxes, leopards, or jaguars. In "were-world," this is known as shape shifting.

Where did the expression "GOING BANANAS" come from?

We say someone is "going bananas" when they're being silly or ridiculous. Monkeys can act pretty crazy, swinging from trees, whooping and calling—and they do love bananas. So, "going bananas" is the human version of all this monkey business.

| Buddhism | Christianity | Hinduism | Islam | Judaism | Taoism |

How many religions are there in the world?

The religions that are most organized, and that have the most followers today, are Buddhism, Christianity, Hinduism, Islam, Judaism, and Taoism. That makes six, but there are many other religions practiced around the world.

What is the Parthenon?

A surviving building of the ancient world. The Parthenon is a temple in Athens, Greece, built in the fifth century B.C. to honor Athena, goddess of war, peace, and wisdom. It stands on a hill called the Acropolis, which overlooks the city. Many of the sculptures from the Parthenon are considered among the world's greatest works of art.

Who invented the YO-YO?

Yo-yos were known in ancient China and Greece, but the Philippines put the yo-yo on the modern map. In the 16th century, Filipinos used yo-yos to snare animal prey from trees. As you can imagine, Filipinos became very good yo-yo players! In 1920, American Donald F. Duncan saw a Filipino man yo-yoing. Soon after, Duncan went into the yo-yo business and made it the world's most famous toy. Since then, going "Around the World" has become a well-known maneuver. In 1992, a yo-yo went aboard the space shuttle Atlantis and traveled 3,321,007 miles—going around the world, for real, 127 times!

What is Dr. Seuss's REAL NAME?

Theodor Seuss Geisel (1904–1991)—better known as Dr. Seuss, the Pulitzer prize-winning author of 47 children's books. His work takes place in a silly make-believe world filled with truffula trees, ziffs and zuffs, and nerkles and nerds, but each book has something to say to adults and children about real life. "I like nonsense," Dr. Seuss has said. "It wakes up the brain cells." Among his most famous books are *The Cat in the Hat, Green Eggs and Ham,* and *How the Grinch Stole Christmas.*

WHY DO WE BREATHE?

We breathe because every cell in the body needs oxygen from the air to stay alive. When air comes into the lungs, oxygen is passed into the bloodstream. The bloodstream carries oxygen to the cells. Along the way, blood picks up waste called carbon dioxide and returns it to the lungs, where it is breathed out. Breathing is automatic—we don't have to think about it. You take about 20,000 breaths a day, which could add up to over 600 million in your lifetime.

How is RUBBER made?

I'M A BIG SAP!

Natural rubber comes from the sap of certain trees, and synthetic rubber is made by people. Rubber trees are found mostly in tropical climates. To make the trees' sap into a useful product called *latex*, water is removed and chemicals are added. The latex is then rolled into rubber sheets. Synthetic rubber is made from coal, oil, and natural gas. Rubber is one of the most useful products in the world. It holds air and keeps out moisture. It's elastic and durable. Some of the rubber products we use are tires, boots, raincoats, balls, erasers, and, of course, rubber bands!

Who was the youngest ruler of a nation?

A two-year-old boy, Emperor Hsuan T'ung, the last emperor of China. He was born in 1906. Just six years later, a revolution swept the country and everything changed. Henry P'u-i, as the young emperor was known, was forced to leave China. He did return, but was put in jail. Finally, for the 10 years before he died in 1967, T'ung was allowed to work as a gardener at one of the colleges in Beijing, the capital of China. So, at the end of his life, the last emperor was ruled by others.

WHAT IS THE FASTEST TRAIN?

The TGV (Train à Grande Vitesse), a high-speed electric train system in France. There are more than 350 trains that run on the TGV. The fastest one, so far, is the Atlantique. Its average cruising speed is 186 miles per hour. The company is planning an even speedier version. The TGV 2000 is expected to cruise at 217 miles per hour.

I'M ALMOST FASTER THAN A SPEEDING BULLET!

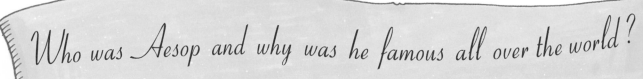

Who was Aesop and why was he famous all over the world?

DO YOU WANT TO RACE?

Aesop was a Greek storyteller who lived from about 620 to 560 B.C. Since then, his fables have circled the world. Fables tell us about human behavior. In *The Tortoise and the Hare*, the two animals run a race. The speedy rabbit is so sure of winning that he takes his time and even naps. But the slow tortoise "keeps on trucking" and wins the race. Aesop's moral, or lesson, is that determination and steady work will get you where you want to go every time.

SURE! HO-HUM.

READY? SET? GO!!

HOW DO TERMITES BUILD A MOUND?

Termites build big homes called "mounds" by cementing bits of soil together with their saliva. There are many different types of termites, but the big builders live in colonies that can have millions of members. Their mounds can be 20 to 30 feet high, filled with a maze of tunnels and chambers. Each colony has workers, soldiers, and a king and queen who live in a central chamber. The queen is enormous compared to the others. Her job is to lay thousands of eggs a day. Such termites are most common in warm regions in Africa, Australia, and South America.

IT'S A LOT OF WORK!

What is LEVITATION?

WOW!

HOW TO DO MAGIC

IT WORKS!

ZIP!

Have you ever seen a magician float a person in the air? That's levitation. How is it done? It's the magician's secret, but you can be sure it's a trick. Some people, however, believe we can use mind power to make people or objects levitate. The closest most people come to levitating is floating in a swimming pool!

WHAT IS THE WORLD'S SMALLEST COUNTRY?

It's a country within a city within a country. Vatican City in Rome, Italy, is an independent country governed by the Roman Catholic Church. The Pope lives there. Its total area is only one fifth of a square mile, a distance you could easily walk.

ITALY

VATICAN CITY

Why do stars twinkle?

They really don't. Starlight passes through our atmosphere, and that's where the "twinkling" begins. Dust, smoke, and other particles are always dancing about in the atmosphere. All those swirling particles interfere with a star's light. The star appears to dim and brighten. Also, the atmosphere bends, or *refracts*, the light rays. These influences create the special effect we call twinkling.

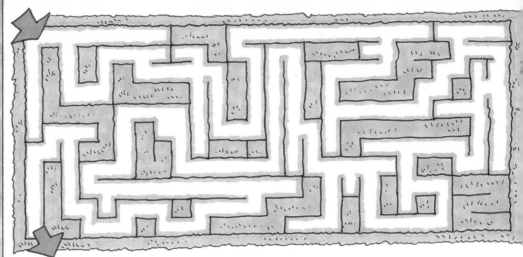

WHAT IS THE WORLD'S LARGEST MAZE?

The world's largest maze was made in a cornfield in Shippensburg, Pennsylvania, in 1995. It covered 172,225 square feet and its zigzag path was 2.03 miles long. But it didn't last. It took only about two months for the grass to grow back.

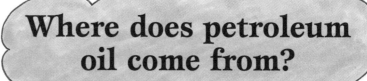

Where does petroleum oil come from?

Underground. Scientists believe that ancient plants and marine organisms are the source of petroleum. As the sea life decomposed, it became trapped in rocks or covered with mud at the bottom of the sea. Over millions of years, carbon and other substances left behind formed oil. Much of the world's petroleum has been found in the Middle East. Petroleum oil is still being formed, but not as fast as the world uses it up.

OIL!

Who made the Statue of Liberty?

Frederic Bartholdi designed the statue and Alexandre Eiffel (who designed the Eiffel Tower) built the framework. The grand lady with the torch was given to the United States by France as a symbol of friendship. It represents the liberty of living under a free form of government. Constructed and shipped to the United States in parts, the statue was erected on Liberty Island in New York Harbor in 1886. *Liberty Enlightening the World* (her full name) is one of the largest statues in the world. It's more than 151 feet, from the sandals to the top of the torch, and weighs 450,000 pounds.

HOW DOES A FIGURE SKATER SPIN AROUND *SO FAST?*

Changing one type of posture to another increases the "rotation rate," or speed of a spin. Say a skater is spinning with her arms outstretched—then she pulls her arms in close to her body. She's going to spin faster because the *momentum,* or energy, from her limbs is passed on to her body.

185

INDEX

Who was Sitting Bull? • **What makes rainbows appear?** • **What is virtual reality?** •

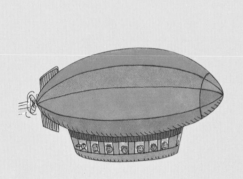 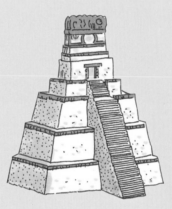 

How do you travel light? • **Who were the Maya?** • **What's at the center of Earth?** •

Who was Mozart? • **Is a four-leaf clover lucky?** • **Why do apes groom each other?** •

Do vampires really exist? • **What are robots used for?** • **Do animals use tools?** •